THE AUTOBIOGRAPHY

OF ST. THÉRÈSE

OF LISIEUX

THE AUTOBIOGRAPHY

OF ST. THÉRÈSE

OF LISIEUX

THE STORY OF A SOUL

TRANSLATED

WITH AN INTRODUCTION

BY JOHN BEEVERS

IMAGE BOOKS | DOUBLEDAY

New York   London   Toronto   Sydney   Auckland

AN IMAGE BOOK
PUBLISHED BY DOUBLEDAY
a division of Random House, Inc.
1540 Broadway, New York, New York 10036

IMAGE, DOUBLEDAY, and the portrayal of a deer drinking
from a stream are trademarks of Doubleday, a division of
Random House, Inc.

First Image edition published September 1957
by special arrangement with Doubleday.
This Image edition published August 2001.

Nihil Obstat:
John A. Goodwine, J.C.D., Censor Librorum
Imprimatur:
Francis Cardinal Spellman, Archbishop of New York
May 24, 1957

ISBN 0-385-02903-9
Library of Congress Catalog Card Number: 57-10467
Copyright © 1957 by Doubleday, a division of Random House, Inc.
Preface copyright © 2001 by Patrick Ahern

INTRODUCTION

At half past eleven on the night of January 2, 1873, Marie Françoise Thérèse Martin was born at Alençon, a small town in the north of France.

Just under twenty-five years later, at about twenty minutes past seven on the evening of September 30, 1897, she died, a nun, in the infirmary of the Carmel of Lisieux, another town in Normandy.

Only a handful of people knew anything of her during her short life, for she entered Carmel when she was fifteen, and few knew or cared that she was dead.

Now she is known and venerated throughout the world as St. Thérèse of the Child Jesus.

She was canonised by Pius XI on May 17, 1925, a mere twenty-eight years after her death. The next year she was declared, with St. Francis Xavier, the principal patron of all missionaries and missions. Later she was declared the secondary patron of France with St. Joan of Arc.

Never has there been an apotheosis so swift and so complete. It is an amazing business no matter how one looks at it. We have this girl born into an obscure middle-class family in a small provincial town; there was nothing apparently remarkable about her intelligence; in her early years she was very shy and moody; and, to crown it all, she vanished behind a convent wall at the age of fifteen and died a few years later. Yet now she is invoked by millions every day and her statue stands in thousands of churches.

How has it happened? Well, it is, of course, essentially the work of God, but God does not reject very ordinary means to accomplish His will. Here He shows a book, the book which follows this introduction. As Benedict XV said, St. Thérèse could not have fulfilled her mission "without the world-wide circulation of *The Story of a Soul*."

I will return to this book, but first I must give a few more details of her life and surroundings which she does not give.*

Her father, Louis Martin, was a watchmaker by trade. In his youth he believed he had a vocation to the monastic life, but when he was thirty-five, he married a young woman of Alençon, Zélie Marie Guérin. She was a lacemaker and she, too, had sought to enter religion. They had nine children. Two boys and two girls died in infancy, and they were left with five daughters. Their last child was Thérèse and for a time it seemed that she would die. Soon after her birth she had to leave Alençon and stay for a year with a wet nurse in a nearby hamlet. This stay in the country turned her into a lively,

---

* I have told the full story in *Storm of Glory* (Doubleday Image Books, Garden City, New York, 1955).

healthy child. From her own story we see in what reverence and affection she held her parents, but it is perhaps not fully realised just how great a part the teaching and example of her father and mother played in her life. In all unessential matters they were a narrow-minded couple and we should find their taste in art and literature deplorable. Neither Alençon nor Lisieux was at that time a particularly gay place—using "gay" in its worldly sense. But the Martin family and their relatives, the Guérins, took no part in what little gaiety there was. Louis and Zélie Martin concerned themselves with three things and three things only—the Church, their family, and their work. Suitable recreation had, of course, its place in their lives, but no time was wasted in chasing so-called pleasures. Nowadays such a life seems to many far too narrow and circumscribed. Yet a life spent in serving God and performing all the duties of one's state in life is immeasurably fuller, richer, and happier than one passed in worldly activities. Such was the life the Martins led and so it was a wholly Christian life. There was nothing narrow or provincial about the Christianity of the Martins. Their dress, their manners, their vocabulary, and their tastes were all unsmart and unfashionable, but how unimportant that is when we consider the depth, the passion, and the vitality of their religious life. Thérèse never had to unlearn anything about the Christian way of life after her entry into Carmel. All she had seen and heard of it in her natural family remained valid when she joined the supernatural family of Carmel. As she grew older, her prayers and meditation and her life of heroic sanctity brought her a steadily deepening spiritual insight, but her soul saw nothing different from what it had seen during its early, formative years. It saw more clearly and understood more fully—that is all.

It must not be thought that the childhood of Thérèse was in any way dull or repressed. It was full of fun. Her autobiography is *The*

Story of a Soul and so, very naturally, it omits many of the ordinary, everyday details of her life. When she was fifteen, she wrote: "I want to be a saint." She has magnificently fulfilled this desire. But when this saint was a child, she went for holidays to the seaside and enjoyed shrimping and donkey rides. She kept silkworms, rabbits, doves, a magpie, and goldfish, and a spaniel called Tom was a special favourite of hers. She was a great mimic and entertained her family with her imitations of people they knew. Her life was holy; it was never marred by false piety. She was good but never priggish. Yet running parallel with all these usual external activities of normal childhood was an intense spiritual life. We all know, of course, that St. Thérèse lived for only twenty-four years, but though we know this, we still too often fail to appreciate her astonishing precocity in spiritual affairs. We can read a letter she wrote to her cousin in the summer of 1887 when she was fourteen. Its main news is that eight of her silkworms had died and it is a typical letter of a fourteen-year-old girl, quite trivial and slightly facetious. Yet, that same summer, as she tells in *The Story of a Soul*, this experience happened to her:

"One Sunday when I was looking at a picture of Our Lord on the Cross, I saw the Blood coming from one of His hands, and I felt terribly sad to think that It was falling to the earth and that no one was rushing forward to catch It. I determined to stay continually at the foot of the Cross and receive it. I knew that I should then have to spread It among other souls. The cry of Jesus on the Cross—'I am thirsty'—rang continually in my heart and set me burning with a new, intense longing. I wanted to quench the thirst of my Well-Beloved and I myself was consumed with a thirst for souls. I was concerned not with the souls of priests but with those of great sinners which I wanted to snatch from the flames of hell."

It is a far cry from silkworms.

Not only was she incredibly precocious in her spirituality. Her character and her will were strong and resolute at a time when most of us are suffering from all the weaknesses and uncertainties of early adolesence. The story of her appeal to Leo XIII is so familiar that we have ceased to be astonished by it. Yet if we pause and consider it for a moment, we shall see how remarkable it was. We have a girl, not yet fifteen, who has been reared in a small provincial town and is quite without worldly experience. She is suddenly whisked off across France and Switzerland and arrives in Rome. There, in the midst of all the outward majesty of the Vatican and fully conscious of the greatness of Leo XIII, both as a man and as the Vicar of Christ, she does not allow her natural nervousness and awe to deflect her from her purpose. She had gone to Rome to plead her cause with the Pope and no human considerations could prevent her.

I know that St. Thérèse is known everywhere as the Little Flower and that it was the name she gave herself. It is no doubt presumptuous of me to say that I do not care for it. My dislike of it is of no importance whatsoever, but I think my reasons for my dislike are. When St. Thérèse calls herself a little flower, she is using one of her many images to describe her relationship to God and it is a most suitable one. But I believe that if we think of her only as a little flower, we do her grave disservice. It is a phrase which can create a very false image of her. It creates a picture of weakness, of frailty, and of helplessness. Now that is a true enough picture when we compare any creature with its Creator, but we must be very careful not to let this title mislead us about the quality of St. Thérèse's character. It was more like an oak tree than a little flower. Her will was of steel. Very early in life she decided to become a saint and fixed her love upon God to the exclusion of all else. Nothing made her deviate an inch from her chosen path. People with this inflexibility of will are often unpleasant. That, however, is because the end to which their will directs itself is not a good and proper end. But if the will is directed solely to God, all harshness, all selfishness, and all the signs of a firm but ill-directed will vanish, for the will is turned against all the manifestations of unregenerate human nature. Its strength is used to destroy them. So it was with St. Thérèse. It is quite certain that had we met St. Thérèse we should have noticed nothing remarkable about her. Many of the nuns who lived with her thought of her as a nice little thing—nothing more. For she gave no impression of her tremendous strength. Yet her nature was a violent one. Her mother said of her: "She flings herself into the most dreadful rages when things don't go as she wants them. She rolls on the ground as if she's given up hope of anything ever being right again. Sometimes she's so overcome that she chokes." As she grew up, this violence was brought under control and the violence of anger became the violence of love. So, if we must, let us call her the Little Flower in affection, remembering always that it is a name which bears no relation at all to the character of St. Thérèse.

Let us now consider the book St. Thérèse wrote. The idea of writing it was not her own. On a winter evening at the beginning of 1895, two and a half years before she died, she was talking to her sisters Marie and Pauline—the latter was then prioress. She recalled some incidents of her childhood, and Marie suggested to Pauline that Thérèse should write an account of her early life. Pauline, in her capacity as prioress, gave Thérèse a formal order to do this. Rarely can a masterpiece have been written under conditions such as this was. Like all the other nuns in Carmel, Thérèse worked hard all day. Her only free time was a short spell in the evening. Then she sat on her stool in her cold cell and, with a notebook on her knee, scribbled away by the dim light of a little oil lamp. She wrote it without making any division into chapters; Pauline made this division later when the manuscript was being prepared for printing. This division has been followed in this translation. When she read the manuscript, Pauline considered it incomplete, as Thérèse's life in religion was hardly touched on. But by then Mother Marie of Gonzaga had become prioress. She was eminently unfitted to hold that position because of her unstable, neurotic character, and Pauline dared say nothing to her about Thérèse's manuscript. However, Thérèse became seriously ill and this induced Pauline to speak. She told Mother Marie of what she, when prioress, had ordered Thérèse to write and suggested that, as Thérèse was going to die before long, it would be as well for her to write about her life in Carmel. She made the point that such a document would be useful when the time came to write Thérèse's *circulaire*, that account of a Carmelite nun which is sent to other Carmels after her death. Mother Marie of Gonzaga agreed, and Thérèse was ordered to continue her story. She began work on it in June, 1897, and this section comprises chapters nine and ten. It was finished early in July. Thérèse was only a few weeks from death as she wrote. She lay in her invalid carriage under the chestnut trees in the Carmel garden and wrote as novices came to talk to her, and every nun who passed stopped for a word.

The last chapter in the original printed version of her manuscript was written before that portion addressed to Mother Marie of Gonzaga. Her eldest sister, Marie, asked her to set down the secrets Jesus had revealed to her. Thérèse obeyed during September, 1896.

A month before she died Thérèse told Pauline: "What I have written will do a lot of good. It will make the kindness of God better known."

How did this obscure manuscript written by an obscure nun at the bidding of three different people ever come to the printing press? It was Pauline who suggested to Mother Marie of Gonzaga that it should be printed. Mother Marie agreed, provided that it should be made to appear that the complete manuscript was addressed to her. She sent the manuscript to a local prior who had given retreats at the Carmel and who knew Thérèse personally. He approved it wholeheartedly, although he thought its grammar needed correcting and its style polishing, and he obtained the imprimatur of the Bishop of Bayeux. On September 30, 1898, the manuscript was published in an edition of two thousand copies. A prioress of a well-known Carmel read it and declared: "Age and experience would have changed her opinions about spiritual matters." Another prioress said: "The thought that this manuscript is now free for anyone to read distresses me beyond words." These were not typical reactions and the book sold steadily. In the first twelve years forty-seven thousand copies were sold. Beween 1910 and 1915 a hundred and sixty-four thousand copies were bought. Today millions of copies have spread throughout the world and it has been translated into thirty-eight languages. It is the great best seller of this century. Yet at first sight there is nothing extraordinary about it, nothing to warrant this phenomenal success. *The Story of a Soul* is not a great literary work. As literature it cannot be compared with St. Augustine's *Confessions*, with St. Teresa's autobiography, or with St. Francis de Sales's *Introduction to a Devout Life*. It often happens that anyone reading *The Story of a Soul* for the first time will be quite unimpressed and may even find it distasteful because it is written in the idiom of an age which, though near us in time, is emotionally far distant from us. But it is very certain that this reader will not forget it and that, one day, he will return to it and read it again—and again. Once read, it cannot be forgotten. And the range of its appeal is tremendous: simple, ill-educated people and great scholars read it. It is a book which moves peasants and popes. Men and women of every race and of every kind of intelligence and education succumb to its spell. Holy Scripture apart—and Holy Scripture is on a wholly different plane from any other book—no other book, whether it is concerned with secular or spiritual matters, has this universality of appeal. This, I am aware, is a big claim to make and it may be dismissed as a piece of pious exaggeration. Yet it is literally true. It is a baffling phenomenon. We can understand clearly and exactly why *Robinson Crusoe* and *Alice in Wonderland* hold the position they do in the Western world, but it is very hard to see the reason for the world-wide fame of St. Thérèse's book. Yet it is a great book, an unforgettable book, and a book whose influence deepens and widens every year. We go wrong, I think, because we judge it by normal and natural standards. But it is not a normal or a natural book. It is abnormal because it is a supernatural book. In the words of Pius XI, St. Thérèse "attained to the knowledge of supernatural things in such abundant measure that she was able to point out the sure way of salvation to others," and it is in *The Story of a Soul* that she points out this sure way. As St. Thérèse sat in her cell and wrote, her companion was the Holy Ghost. Her book was divinely inspired, not, it must be understood, as Holy Scripture is inspired, but inspired as perhaps no other book has been. That is why when we read it its obvious faults—when we judge it by purely literary standards—mean nothing. They are unimportant and irrelevant. Beneath its occasional verbal infelicities, the few passages of saccharine sweetness, and all the italics and exclamation marks, there burns a fierce, exultant flame of holy passion, and it is this passion which grips the reader—sometimes at once, but nearly always after a second or third reading.

When we pick up *The Story of a Soul* we are handling something akin to a miracle. We have a book which was never written as a book. It was scribbled very quickly and produced in three parts, each addressed to a different person. Much of it was written when its author knew she was dying and was suffering all the pain and distress of a fatal illness. Now it is the most widely read book of spirituality in the world and is acclaimed by popes for the sureness of its teaching.

What is this teaching? It is not complicated, nor is it new. Many books have been written about it, but during the last year or two I have seen signs that it is being realised that too much subtlety and ingenuity have been expended in examining the doctrine of St. Thérèse, and that she is not best served by a proliferation of learned volumes bristling with footnotes. What St. Thérèse does is to throw into relief certain truths already divinely revealed and to insist on their vital importance. These truths have always been known by Christendom but, though known and accepted, they have often been neglected. Indeed, as far as some of the truths of Christ's teaching are concerned, one has to look back across many centuries before finding anyone who enunciates them with the boldness and emphasis of St. Thérèse. So, though her teaching is not really new, it has about it the freshness and the force of a rediscovery.

She called her doctrine "the little way of spiritual childhood," and it is based on complete and unshakeable confidence in God's love for us. This confidence means that we cannot be afraid of God even though we sin, for we know that, being human, sin we shall but, provided that after each fall, we stumble to our feet again and continue our advance to God, He will instantly forgive us and come to meet us. St. Thérèse does not minimise the gravity of sin, but she insists that we must not be crushed by it. We must repent and realise that God's love never fails. And God's love for us must be matched, within our human limitations, by our love for Him. There must be a ceaseless flow of love—to and fro—between Creator and creature.

Now this interchange of love does away with the feeling that to please God we must do great and extraordinary things. If we only fear God, we are in danger of deluding ourselves that He needs to be placated by deeds which, in some measure, match His awful majesty. Few saints have appreciated this majesty better than St. Thérèse, but she is never overawed by it. She accepts it and accepts, too, the fact of her own littleness by the side of it. She knows that nothing she can ever do can be adequate, but this leaves her quite untroubled. The depth of her love for God means that all the small, trivial acts of which she is capable take on great value because of the motive behind them. And God, with His overwhelming love and understanding, accepts them joyfully. So "the little way" means that salvation is made not easy, but obviously possible. Salvation has, of course, always been possible, but from time to time there have arisen within the Church movements such as Jansenism which belittled or denied God's mercy. The Church has invariably condemned such movements, but these heresies have left their mark and men have been plunged in despair, believing that they could never achieve salvation, that a life of unbelievable austerity and heroic deeds was essential, and that without such a life they were of no account before God. This is rank heresy. The whole teaching of the Church condemns it. But vestiges of it still survived.

Then Thérèse arrived and lived and taught her little way. And at once the Church saw that God had raised up a saint to sweep away the last traces of this false fear of God and three popes have ratified her words and example.

The last words St. Thérèse uttered, a second or two before she died, were: "Oh! I love Him! . . . My God. . . . I love You!" Her little way of spiritual childhood has made countless thousands utter the same passionate cry of love and adoration. And that is the measure of her greatness and the greatness of this book.

THE AUTOBIOGRAPHY

OF ST. THÉRÈSE

OF LISIEUX

CHAPTER ONE

I am going to entrust the story of my soul to you, my darling Mother, to you who are doubly my mother. When you asked me to do this, I felt it might be too great a distraction and might make me too concerned about myself, but afterwards Jesus made me realise that I should please Him by unquestioning obedience. Besides, it involves me in only one thing: to start extolling now the mercies of the Lord—which I shall go on doing throughout eternity.

Before starting, I knelt before the statue of Mary, the one which has given us so many proofs that the Queen of Heaven looks after us like a mother. I begged her to guide my hand so that I should not write a line that would displease her. Then I opened the Gospels and saw these words: "Then He went up onto the mountainside, and called to Him those whom it pleased Him to call." There, indeed, was the mystery of my vocation, of my whole life, and of the special graces given me by Jesus. He does not call those who are worthy, but those He chooses. As St. Paul says: "I will show pity, He tells Moses, on those whom I pity; I will show mercy where I am merciful; the effect comes, then, from God's mercy, not from man's will, or man's alacrity."

I had wondered for a long time why God had preferences and why all souls did not receive an equal amount of grace. I was astonished to see how He showered extraordinary favours on saints who had sinned against Him, saints such as St. Paul and St. Augustine. He forced them, as it were, to accept His graces. I was just as astonished when I read the lives of saints to see that Our Lord cherished certain favoured souls from the cradle to the grave and never allowed any kind of obstacle to check their flight towards Him. He bestowed such favours on them that they were unable to tarnish the spotless splendour of their baptismal robe. I also wondered why such vast numbers of poor savages died before they had even heard the name of God.

Jesus saw fit to enlighten me about this mystery. He set the book of nature before me and I saw that all the flowers He has created are lovely. The splendour of the rose and the whiteness of the lily do not rob the little violet of its scent nor the daisy of its simple charm. I realised that if every tiny flower wanted to be a rose, spring would lose its loveliness and there would be no wild flowers to make the meadows gay.

It is just the same in the world of souls—which is the garden of Jesus. He has created the great saints who are like the lilies and the roses, but He has also created much lesser saints and they must be content to be the daisies or the violets which rejoice His eyes whenever He glances down. Perfection consists in doing His will, in being that which He wants us to be.

I also understood that God's love shows itself just as well in the simplest soul which puts up no resistance to His grace as it does in the loftiest soul. Indeed, as it is love's nature to humble itself, if all souls were like those of the holy doctors who have illumined the Church with the light of their doctrine, it seems that God would not have stooped low enough by entering their hearts. But God has created the baby who knows nothing and can utter only feeble cries. He has created the poor savage with no guide but natural law, and it is to their hearts that He deigns to stoop. They are His wild flowers whose homeliness delights Him. By stooping down to them, He manifests His infinite grandeur. The sun shines equally both on cedars and on every tiny flower. In just the same way God looks after every soul as if it had no equal. All is planned for the good of every soul, exactly as the seasons are so arranged that the humblest daisy blossoms at the appointed time.

I'm sure, darling Mother, that you are wondering where I am heading, for so far I've said nothing about the story of my life. But you did ask me to write freely about whatever came into my head. So—to be quite accurate—I am not going to write "my life," but put down "my thoughts" about the graces God has given me.

I have now reached a stage in my life when I can glance back at the past, for my soul has matured in a crucible of inner and external trials. Now, like a flower braced by a storm, I can raise my head and see that the words of the Psalmist have been fulfilled in me: "The Lord is my shepherd; how can I lack anything? He gives me a resting place where there is green pasture, leads me out to the cool water's brink, refreshed and content . . . dark be the valley about my path, but I fear none while he is with me." For me, the Lord has always been "pitying and gracious, patient and rich in mercy." So, Mother, it is with joy that I shall sing to you of His mercies. As it is for you alone that I am going to write the story of the Little Flower gathered by Jesus, I shall speak quite freely, without worrying about style or all the digressions I'm sure to make. A mother always understands her child even though it can lisp only a few words. So I am sure you will understand me, as it was you who fashioned my soul and offered it to Jesus.

I believe that if a little flower could speak, it would tell very simply and fully all that God had done for it. It would not say that it was ungraceful and had no scent, that the sun had spoilt its freshness, or that a storm had snapped its stem—not when it knew the exact opposite was true.

The flower who is now going to tell her story rejoices at having to relate all the kindnesses freely done her by Jesus. She is well aware that there was nothing about her to attract His attention, and that it is His mercy alone which has created whatever there is of good in her. It was He who ensured that she began to grow in a most pure and holy soil, and it was He who saw to it that eight fair white lilies came before her. His love made Him want to keep His little flower safe from the tainted breezes of the world, and so she had scarcely begun to unfold her petals before He transplanted her on to the mountain of Carmel.

I have, Mother, just summed up in a few words what God has done for me. Now I am going to give some details of my life as a child. I know that you, with your mother's heart, will find it not without charm, though it might bore anyone else. For the memories I'm going to recall are yours as well, since my childhood was spent close to you and our saintly parents surrounded us both with the same tenderness and care. May they bless the least of their children and help her to sing of the divine mercy!

I separate into three very distinct periods the story of my soul until I entered Carmel. The first, though short, is full of memories. It stretches from the time I began to reason until our beloved mother left us for heaven.

God favoured me by awakening my intelligence very early and by imprinting the happenings of my childhood so sharply on my memory that the things I am going to write about seem as if they took place yesterday. No doubt Jesus, in His love, wanted to make me know and appreciate the incomparable mother he had given me, as He was in haste to crown her in heaven.

Throughout the whole of my life God has been pleased to surround me with love. My first memories are of smiles and loving caresses. He placed me in the midst of great love and He also put a similar love in my little heart and made it sensitive and affectionate. So I loved Daddy and Mummy very much and, as I was very openhearted, I showed my love in a thousand ways. Some of them were rather queer, as you can see from this extract from one of Mummy's letters: "Baby is a unique little imp. She has just been hugging me and wishing me dead! 'Oh, how I wish, darling Mummy, that you would die!' I scolded her. She said: 'It's so that you can go to heaven, for you say that one has to die to go there.' When she is overcome by love for her father, she wishes he were dead too. The little darling never wants to leave me. She always keeps near me and loves to go into the garden, but if I'm not there she won't stay and cries so much that she has to be brought to me."

Here is a passage from another letter: "The other day little Thérèse asked me if she would go to heaven. 'Yes,' I told her, 'if you are very good.' 'Yes, but if I were naughty I should go to hell and I know very well what I should do there. I should fly up to you in heaven and then you'd hug me very tight. How could God take me away from you then?' From the look on her face I saw that she was quite sure that God could do nothing to her if she hid herself in her mother's arms. Everyone has to know the moment she's done the slightest thing wrong. Yesterday she accidentally tore a bit of the wallpaper and she was really terribly upset and wanted to tell her father about it as soon as possible. We had forgotten all about it when he came in four hours later, but she ran to Marie at once and said: 'Tell Daddy straightway that I tore the paper.' She stood there like a criminal waiting to be sentenced, but she thinks she'll be forgiven more easily if she accuses herself."

I loved my dear godmother very much. Without seeming to, I took notice of all that was done and said around me, and I think I had the same opinions then as now. I listened very attentively when she was teaching Céline, and I behaved very well and did everything she told me in order to be allowed into the room during these lessons. And so she gave me lots of presents which delighted me, though they weren't at all valuable.

I was very proud of my two big sisters, but it was you, Pauline, who were my ideal. When I was beginning to talk and Mummy used to ask me: "What are you thinking about?" my reply was always the same: "Of Pauline." I used to hear it said that you were certain to become a nun and, though I wasn't too sure what this meant, I thought: "And I too will be a nun." This is one of the first things I remember, and I never wavered in my resolution. It was your example which drew me to the Spouse of Virgins from the time I was two. How many tender memories I could disclose to you, but I must go on with the full story of the Little Flower, for if I were to write in detail about my relations with you I should have to leave all the rest of my story.

Darling Léonie was also very dear to me and she loved me greatly. In the evenings she used to look after me when the rest of the family went out for a walk, and I can still hear her sweet voice singing the little songs that sent me off to sleep. I remember her first Communion very well. I was put to bed early in the evening, as I was too young to stay up for the celebration dinner, but I can still see Daddy coming up to me and bringing his little queen a piece of the first-Communion cake.

Now I have only to tell of Céline, the little companion of my childhood, and I have so many memories of her that I don't know which to chose. We understood each other perfectly, but I was much livelier and far less artless. Although I was three and a half years younger, I thought of us as the same age. Here is a passage from one of Mummy's letters which will show you Céline's goodness and my naughtiness: "Céline seems naturally good. Goodness is embedded in her very being. Her soul is guileless and has a horror of evil. But I can't be too sure how the little minx will turn out, for she's such a little madcap. She is more intelligent than Céline, but nothing like as gentle and she is stubborn beyond words. It's quite impossible to budge her when she says no. Putting her in the cellar for a whole day would not make her say yes. She'd sooner sleep there. Yet she has a heart of gold and is very affectionate and without a trace of slyness. It's amusing to see her coming running to me to confess her faults: 'Mummy, I've given Céline a push and I've thumped her, but I won't do it again'. She says that every time she has done anything wrong."

I had a fault of which Mummy says nothing in her letters: great self-love. I could give several examples if it would not make my story too long. Mummy said to me one day: "Thérèse, I'll give you a halfpenny if you will kiss the ground." This was quite a fortune to me. I should not have had to bend far to get it, for, as I was little, there wasn't much space between my face and the ground. But my pride revolted, so, holding myself very straight, I said: "Oh no, Mummy, I'd rather not have the halfpenny."

Another time we were going out to visit a friend. Mummy told Marie to put me in my pretty blue dress trimmed with lace, but to see that my arms were covered to keep the sun off them. I let myself be dressed with the indifference that children should have at that age, but I thought I should have been much prettier with bare arms.

With such a temperament I should have become very wicked and perhaps have been eternally lost if I had been brought up by bad parents. But Jesus watched over me. He drew good from my faults, for, checked in good time, they served to make me grow in perfection. As I loved myself and also loved goodness, I had only to be told once that something was not good. I am pleased to see from Mummy's letters that I became more of a consolation to her as I grew older. As I was surrounded by nothing but good examples, I naturally wished to imitate them. Here's what she wrote in 1876: "Now even Thérèse wants to start making sacrifices. Marie has given her two little sisters some beads on which to count their acts of self-denial. They often talk of spiritual things. The other day Céline said: 'How can God be in such a tiny Host?' Thérèse told her: 'That's not so amazing as God is almighty.' 'What does almighty mean?' 'Why, it means He can do whatever He wants.' She and Céline are very fond of each other and amuse themselves together. Every evening after dinner Céline goes off to catch their bantam cock and hen. They bring them in and sit by the fire and play with them for hours. One morning Thérèse climbed out of her bed and joined Céline in hers. When Louise came to dress her, Thérèse hugged and kissed her sister and said: 'Leave me alone, Louise, for we are just like the bantams. We can't be separated.' "

It is very true that I could not settle without Céline. I would leave the table before finishing my dessert rather than not follow her when she left. I twisted about in my high chair in my eagerness to get down quickly, and then we would go off and play together.

On Sundays Mummy stayed at home to look after me, as I was too young to go to Mass. I was very good and tip-toed about the house, but the moment I saw the door open I went wild with joy and rushed up to my pretty sister who was dressed in her Sunday best and cried: "Oh, Céline, give me the blessed bread—quickly, quickly!" Once she hadn't any, as she'd arrived too late at church. What was to be done? It was impossible for me to do without it, for it was my Mass. I found an answer very quickly. "You haven't any blessed bread! Make some then!" No sooner said than done. Céline jumped on a chair, reached up to the cupboard, took out a loaf, and cut me off a piece. She recited a Hail Mary very solemnly over it and gave me it. I made the sign of the Cross and ate it with great devotion. It tasted exactly like blessed bread.

One day Léonie, no doubt thinking she was too old to play with dolls, came to us both with a basket filled with their clothes, ribbons, and other odds and ends. Her own doll was on top. She said: "Here you are darlings. Take what you want." Céline took a little bundle of silk braid. I thought for a moment, then stretched out my hand and declared "I choose everything," and, without more ado, I carried off the lot. Everyone thought this quite fair.

This episode sums up the whole of my life. Much later, when I understood what perfection was, I realised that to become a saint one must suffer a great deal, always seek what is best, and forget oneself. I understood that there were many kinds of sanctity and that each soul was free to respond to the approaches of Our Lord and to do little or much for Him—in other words, to make a choice among the sacrifices He demands. Then, just as when I was a child, I cried: "My God, I choose all. I do not want to be a saint by halves. I am not afraid to suffer for You. I fear only one thing—that I should keep my own will. So take it, for I choose all that You will."

But I must stop, for I mustn't tell you about my adolescence yet, but about the little four-year-old person. I had a dream then which is deeply impressed on my memory. One night I dreamt that I was going out to walk by myself in the garden. I saw, near the arbour, two horrible little devils on a barrel which stood there. They were astonishingly lively in spite of the heavy chains they had on their feet. Suddenly they glared at me with their blazing eyes; then, looking much more frightened than I was, they jumped down from the barrel and ran to hide in the linen room which was just opposite. When I saw they were such cowards, I wanted to find out what they were up to, so I went to the window. These wretched little imps were running about on the tables and didn't know what to do to escape from my gaze. Every now and then they came and peeped uneasily out of the window, but when they saw I was still there, they began to run about again as if crazy with despair. Of course there was nothing extraordinary about the dream, yet I think God has let me remember it to prove to me that a soul in a state of grace need fear nothing from devils, for they are so cowardly that they flee from the gaze of a child.

How happy I was at that age. I was beginning to enjoy life and I felt the attraction of goodness. I think my character was the same then as now, for I already had very great self-control. How quickly they went, those golden days of my early childhood, yet what lovely memories I have of them. I remember so happily the days we went with Daddy to the Pavilion. I can't forget the slightest detail. I remember above all the walks on Sunday when Mummy always came with us. I can still feel the deep emotion I felt when I saw the fields of wheat starred with poppies, cornflowers, and daisies. I was already in love with far distances, with open spaces, and with great trees.

During these long walks we often met poor people, and I was always entrusted with giving them alms, a task which made me very happy. But Daddy sometimes thought the walk was too long for his little queen and took me home before the others—which I didn't like at all. Whenever this happened, Céline used to fill her basket with daisies and give me them when she got home to console me.

Truly, the whole world smiled on me. My path was strewn with flowers and my own happy temperament also made life pleasant. But a new phase was going to begin. I had to be refined by trials and had to suffer while still a child so that I could be offered to Jesus as soon as possible. Just as the spring flowers begin to grow beneath the snow and open in the first rays of the sun, so the Little Flower of whose memories I write had to pass through the winter of trials.

CHAPTER TWO

Every detail of our mother's illness is still
with me, especially the last weeks she spent
on earth. Céline and I were like two unhappy
little exiles. Every morning a neighbour
came for us and we spent the day with her.
Once we had not had time to say our prayers
before leaving, and on our way Céline whispered to me: "Must we tell her that we have
not said our prayers?" "Oh yes!" I said. So
she mentioned it very nervously to this
neighbour, who said: "Well, of course you
must say them," and left us alone together in
a large room. Céline looked at me and we
said: "This is not what Mummy does. She always prayed with us." Even when we were
playing with other children, we never
stopped thinking of our darling mother.
Céline was once given a lovely apricot but

she whispered to me: "We are not going to eat it, for I'm going to give it to Mummy." But Mother was by then far too ill to eat any earthly fruit. She could be satisfied only in heaven, where she would see the glory of God, and drink that mystic wine of which Jesus spoke at the Last Supper, promising to share it with us in His Father's Kingdom.

The moving ceremony of Extreme Unction impressed me profoundly. We all knelt and I can still see the spot where I knelt by the side of Céline. Father was there as well in tears. Either on the day she died or the day after, he took me in his arms and said: "Come and give your dear mother a last kiss." Without saying a word, I touched her forehead with my lips. I don't remember weeping much, and I spoke to no one about how keenly I felt it all.

I watched and listened without saying anything, and as no one had time to bother about me, I saw a lot they wanted to hide from me. I saw the lid of the coffin and stood looking at it for a long time. I knew what it was, although I hadn't seen one before. I was so small that, although Mummy was short, I had to lift my head to see it all. It seemed huge and grim. Fifteen years later I stood in front of another coffin. That of Mother Geneviève. It was the same size as Mummy's and it brought back the days of my childhood. A host of memories came crowding in. I was the same Thérèse, but I had grown. The coffin seemed small, and there was no need for me to lift my head to see it all. I lifted my gaze now only to contemplate heaven and its joys, for all my trials were over and the winter through which my soul had passed had gone for ever.

On the day when the Church blessed the mortal remains of our mother, who had gone to heaven, God decided to give me another mother on earth and to let me choose her. All five of us were looking sadly at each other when Louise turned to Céline and me and exclaimed: "Poor darlings, you've no mother now!" Céline hurled herself into Marie's arms, crying: "Ah, you be my mummy!" I always used to do what she did, but I turned to you and, as if I could see into the future, I ran to you and cried: "Pauline will be my mummy."

As I wrote earlier, it was at this time that I entered the second period of my life. It was the most unhappy one, especially after you, my second mother, had entered Carmel. This period lasted from when I was four and a half to when I was fourteen. Then I regained the character I had when I was a little child and yet I understood the serious meaning of life.

The moment Mummy died my happy disposition changed completely. I had been lively and cheerful, but I became timid and quiet and a bundle of nerves. A glance was often enough to make me burst into tears. I was only happy if no one took any notice of me, and I couldn't endure being with strangers. I was never cheerful except within the family circle, and there the greatest love and kindness surrounded me. Daddy's affection seemed enriched by a real motherly love, and I felt that both you and Marie were the most tender and self-sacrificing of mothers. God's little flower would never have survived if He had not poured His warmth and light on her. She was still too frail to stand up to rain and storm. She needed warmth, the gently dropping dew and the soft airs of spring. She was never without them, for Jesus gave them to her, even amidst the bleak winter of her suffering.

I wasn't at all upset at leaving Alençon. Children like change and I went cheerfully to Lisieux. I remember the journey and how we arrived at my aunt's in the evening. I can still see Jeanne and Marie waiting for us at the door. Next day we were installed in our new home, Les Buisonnets, a villa in a quiet part of the town and near a very pleasant park. I loved it with its views from the attic windows, its lawn and shrubbery in front, and a big garden at the back. It became the scene of tremendous family happiness. In any other spot I felt an exile and cried because I had lost Mummy. But there I was truly happy.

Every morning you came to me and I said my prayers kneeling at your side. Afterwards I had a reading lesson. "Heaven" was the first word I could read. When my lessons were over, I ran upstairs with my marks to the room where Daddy spent most of his time, and I was delighted when I could tell him: "I've got full marks."

Every afternoon I went for a walk with Daddy and paid a visit to the Blessed Sacrament, going to a different church every day. It was during one of these walks that I entered the Carmel chapel for the first time. Daddy showed me the choir grille and said that nuns lived behind it. It never entered my head that I should be among them in nine years' time.

After our walk we went home and I prepared my next day's lessons. For the rest of the day I played in the garden with Daddy, for I wasn't interested in dolls. I got most fun out of soaking seeds and bits of bark in water and then offering the liquid to Daddy in a pretty little cup. He'd take it and smile and pretend to drink it.

I loved growing flowers in the bit of garden given me by Daddy, and I enjoyed decorating little altars I made in a niche in the wall. When I'd finished, I'd run and fetch Daddy. He went into raptures of admiration to please me as he gazed at what I was sure were masterpieces. I should never end if I were to tell all the thousand and one memories I have of things like this. How can I tell of all the love Daddy showered on his little queen?

I particularly loved the days when my "beloved king" took me with him when he went fishing, for I loved the countryside and its birds and flowers. Sometimes I tried to fish with my little line, but I preferred to sit alone on the grass amid the flowers. Then I used to think very deeply, and though I knew nothing of meditation, my soul entered into a true state of prayer. I heard the murmur of the breeze and sounds from far away. The faint music from the band of the soldiers garrisoned in the town reached me and filled me with a gentle melancholy. Earth seemed a place of exile and I dreamt of heaven. The afternoon went quickly and it was soon time to return home, but before going I ate the snack I had brought in my little basket. But the nice bread and jam you had given me didn't look the same. Its freshness was stale and faded. Then earth seemed an even sadder place, and I realised that only in heaven would I know unclouded joy.

Mentioning clouds reminds me that one day the lovely blue of the sky grew overcast and we heard the rumbling of a storm. Lightning shot through the lowering clouds, and I saw a thunderbolt strike nearby. I wasn't a bit frightened. Indeed, I was full of delight, for it seemed that God was very near to me. Daddy wasn't nearly so happy as his little queen. He wasn't frightened by the storm, but the grass and the big marguerites, which were taller than I was, glistened with raindrops, and there were several fields between us and the road. He was afraid I would be soaked, so, in spite of all his fishing tackle, he carried me off on his back.

During my walks with Daddy he loved to let me give alms to the poor people we met. Once we met a poor old man dragging himself painfully along on crutches. I went to give him a penny, but he didn't seem poor enough to need alms. He gave a sad smile as he looked at me and refused to take my offering. I can't describe what I felt. I had wanted to comfort and help him; I thought that I'd hurt him instead. He must have understood what I felt, for I saw him turn round and smile at me. Daddy had just bought me a cake and I longed to give him it. But I didn't dare. I remembered that I'd been told that on the day of one's first Communion any favour asked would be granted. This comforted me and, although I was then only six, I said to myself: "I will pray for my poor old man at my first Communion." I kept my promise five years later, and I hope that God has answered the prayer He inspired me to offer Him for one of the Church's suffering members.

I loved God intensely and very often I offered Him my heart in words taught me by Mummy. Yet one day—or rather evening—in May, I committed a sin that's well worth being recounted here. It greatly humiliated me and I believe I felt perfect contrition for it. Marie said I was too young to go to the May devotions. I stayed at home with Victoire and made my devotions with her, in front of my little altar which I had decorated myself. Everything on it was so small—candlesticks and flower vases and such—that a couple of wax matches lit it perfectly. Sometimes, but not very often, Victoire gave me a surprise present of two candle ends to save my store of matches. One evening, as we were going to begin our prayers, I said to her: "Victoire, will you begin the *Memorare?* I am going to light the matches." She pretended to begin, but said nothing—only looked at me and laughed. I saw my precious matches burning rapidly away and I then begged her to say the prayers. She still kept silent. I jumped up and, with my usual good temper gone, I stamped furiously and shouted at her, telling her how wicked she was. The poor girl stopped laughing, stared at me in astonishment, and showed me two candle ends hidden under her apron. My tears of rage were followed by tears of real repentance, and I firmly resolved never to let anything like that happen again.

I made my first confession soon afterwards. What a wonderful memory I have of it! How carefully you prepared me! You told me I was going to confess my sins not to a man but to God Himself. I was so absolutely convinced of this that I made my confession full of great faith and I even asked you if I should tell Father Ducellier that I loved him with all my heart since it was God I was going to speak to in his person.

Well instructed in all I had to say and do, I entered the confessional and knelt down, but when Father Ducellier opened the shutter he couldn't see anyone. I was so small that my head came below the arm rest. He told me to stand up. I obeyed at once and turned to face him so that I could see him better. I made my confession like a big girl and received his blessing with great devotion, for you had told me that, at that moment, the tears of Jesus would cleanse my soul. I remember what Father Ducellier said to me. He especially urged me to love the Blessed Virgin, and I determined to redouble my affection for her. I left the confessional happier and more light-hearted than I'd ever been before. After that I went to confession on every big feast day, and every time I went it was a real feast for me.

Feast days! What memories these words bring back! I loved feast days so much. You could explain their real meaning so well that they seemed like days spent in heaven. Best of all, I loved when the Blessed Sacrament was carried in procession, for it gave me such joy to scatter flowers beneath the feet of God. But before letting them fall there, I used to throw them as high as I could and nothing delighted me more than to see my rose petals touch the Monstrance. Even if there were not many of the big feast days, every week brought one that was very dear to me—Sunday. What days those Sundays were! It was the feast of God, the feast of rest. We all set out together to High Mass. All along the road and even in church Daddy's little queen clutched his hand. Her place was by his side, and when we had to move forward for the sermon, it was essential to find two chairs side by side. This was not very hard, for everyone found the sight of this fine old man and his little girl so attractive that people hastened to give us their seats. My uncle, who sat with the church wardens, was always delighted to see us arrive. He called me his little sunbeam. I was not really disturbed by being stared at, and I listened most attentively to the sermons although I didn't understand much of them. One on the Passion, preached by Father Ducellier, was the first I grasped. I was deeply moved by it. After that I always understood every sermon. Whenever the preacher mentioned St. Teresa, Daddy would lean over and whisper: "Listen carefully, my little queen. He is speaking of your holy patron." And, indeed, I did listen carefully, but I used to look more at Daddy than at the preacher because I could read so much in his noble face. His eyes sometimes filled with tears which he tried in vain to check. As he heard the eternal truths, he seemed as if he had already left the earth. Yet his life here was very far from its end. Long years stretched ahead of him before he saw the glories of heaven and the Lord dried the tears of His good and faithful servant.

But to go back to Sundays. This happy day which passed so quickly was tinged with sadness. There was no shadow on my happiness until Compline. Then I thought that the day of rest was nearly over and that next day the ordinary life of work and lessons would start again. I felt like an exile on earth and yearned for the peace of heaven and the eternal Sabbath of our true Fatherland. We used to go for a walk before returning home and, to please my aunt, Daddy used to leave Marie or Pauline with her. I was very pleased when I was allowed to stay too. My greatest pleasure was listening to my uncle talk, but I was quite frightened when he took me on his knee and sang "Bluebeard" in a terrifying voice. Daddy came to collect us. As we walked home, I gazed with delight at the stars shining above. There was one group in particular which filled me with joy, for I noticed that it was in the shape of the letter T. I pointed it out to Daddy and told him that my name was written in heaven. I didn't want to see any more of this dreary world and asked him to guide me. Then, without looking where I was going, I kept my face turned up to the starry sky.

How much there is to tell of our winter evenings—especially Sunday evenings! After playing draughts (checkers), I loved sitting on Daddy's knee with Céline as he sang to us in his pleasant voice or recited religious poems. Then we all said our evening prayers together and the little queen knelt by her king. She had only to gaze at him to know how the saints prayed. You carried me up to bed and I used to say: "Have I been good today? Are the little angels going to watch over me?" You always said yes or I should have spent the whole night in tears. Then you and Marie kissed me good night and left me alone in the dark.

I consider I was most fortunate in my being taught by you to overcome my fears. Sometimes, for example, you sent me to fetch something from a room at the other end of the house. If I hadn't been so well trained, I should have become very timid. As it is, it's very hard to frighten me. I've often wondered how you were able to bring me up with so much love and yet not spoil me. You never passed over a single fault, but you never reproached me without good cause, and I knew that you never changed any of your decisions.

You knew all my intimate thoughts and cleared up all my doubts. I once told you how astonished I was that God does not give equal glory in heaven to all His chosen. I was afraid they were not all equally happy. You made me bring Daddy's big tumbler and put it by the side of my tiny thimble. You filled them both with water and asked me which was the fuller. I told you they were both full to the brim and that it was impossible to put more water in them than they could hold. And so, Mother darling, you made me under-

stand that in heaven God will give His chosen their fitting glory and
that the last will have no reason to envy the first. By such means,
you made me understand the most sublime mysteries and gave my
soul its essential food.

I was terribly happy each year when prize day came round. As
usual, justice was observed and I got only the prizes I had merited. I
stood in front of the assembled family and heard my report read by
"the King of France and Navarre." How my heart beat when I received the prizes and the crown! It was like a foreshadowing of the
Day of Judgment. How marvellous these family parties were! As I
saw Daddy so happy, I could foresee nothing of the great trials
ahead of him. Yet one day God showed me, in a remarkable vision,
a living picture of these trials as if to prepare us for them.

Daddy had gone away for several days and he wasn't due home
for a day or two. It was between two and three o'clock in the afternoon; the sun shone brightly and all nature seemed to rejoice. I was
standing alone by a window looking out into the garden and was
feeling very cheerful. I saw a man in front of the wash house. He
was dressed exactly like Daddy, and was of the same height and
bearing, but he was very bent and aged. His head was covered with
a kind of thick veil. I couldn't make out its colour, but it prevented
me from seeing his face. The man wore a hat similar to Daddy's. I
saw him walk slowly and steadily past my little garden. I was suddenly gripped by a supernatural fear, but then I thought that Daddy
had come back and that he had been hiding to surprise me. I
shouted: "Daddy! Daddy!" in a trembling voice. But the mysterious
figure seemed not to hear me and, without even turning his head,
walked on towards a group of fir trees which divided the main path
of the garden. I expected to see him appear at the other side of
these trees, but this prophetic vision disappeared. All this lasted

only a moment, but it impressed itself so deeply on my soul that even today, after fifteen years, the memory of it is as vivid as was the vision itself.

Marie was with you in a neighbouring room. When she heard me shout: "Daddy!" she felt frightened and, as she's told me since, she sensed that something extraordinary was happening. She ran in to me and, without showing her fear, she asked me why I'd shouted out to Daddy when he was in Alençon. I told her what I had just seen. She tried to comfort me by saying that Victoire had hidden her head in her apron to give me a fright. Victoire was questioned, but swore she had not left the kitchen. But I was convinced that I had seen a man and that that man was the image of Daddy. Finally we all went behind the clump of trees and, when we found nobody there, you told me to think no more of it. That I couldn't do. This mysterious vision came into my imagination time and time again. I very often tried to fathom its meaning and I was quite sure that one day I should know its full significance. That day has been a long time coming, but after fourteen years God Himself has revealed its meaning. It was indeed Daddy I had seen walking along bowed by age. He was wearing the symbol of his great trial over his venerable face and white hairs. Just as the adorable face of Jesus was veiled during His Passion, so had the face of His faithful servant to be veiled during the days of his humiliation so that, in heaven, it could shine with greater glory. God foreshadowed His precious trial to us, just like a father who lets his children glimpse the magnificent future he plans for them and who himself enjoys contemplating the priceless treasure they will inherit.

Why did God grant me this vision? Why did He show a child something she could not understand, something which would have broken her heart if she could have understood it? Why? It's one of those mysteries we shall fathom only in heaven.

But how good God is! How well He fits our trials to our strength! At the time of my vision I could never have endured even the thought of the bitter grief the future held for me. I trembled at the very idea that Daddy could die. He was once standing at the top of a ladder and when he saw me standing right below it, he shouted down: "Move away, darling. If I fall, I shall crush you." But I went closer to the ladder. I thought: "Well, at least if Daddy does fall, I shan't suffer by seeing him die, as I shall be killed with him."

I can't put into words how much I loved Daddy. I admired everything about him. He would discuss his ideas with me as if I were grown up and, in my simplicity, I would tell him that if the government leaders heard him they would make him king and France would be happier than she had ever been. But in my heart of hearts I was pleased—though I reproached myself for being selfish—that I was the only one who knew Daddy so well. I knew that if he became King of France and Navarre, he would be unhappy, for that's the fate of all kings. And—most important of all—he would no longer have been my very own King!

I was six or seven when Daddy took us to Trouville. I shall never forget the impression the sea made on me. I could not take my eyes from it. The majestic roaring of its waves filled me with a sense of the power and majesty of God. I remember once, when we were walking on the beach, a man and his wife came up to Daddy and asked if I was his daughter. They said what a pretty little girl I was. I saw Daddy indicate that they shouldn't flatter me. It was the first time I'd been told I was pretty and I was delighted, although I didn't believe it. For you, darling Mother, had taken the greatest care to see that nothing was allowed near me which might blemish my innocence and that I never heard anything likely to awaken my vanity. As I was accustomed to pay attention only to what you and

Daddy said, I didn't attach much importance to this lady's words and her admiring looks.

I sat with you on a rock one evening at the time when the sun seems to sink into the vastness of the ocean at the end of a path of light. (I remembered the moving story of *The Golden Path*.) I gazed at this path of light and saw it as a symbol of the grace which lit the way along which the little white-sailed skiff would journey. Sitting by your side, Pauline, I resolved never to let my soul wander from the gaze of Jesus, so that it could sail peacefully towards the shores of heaven.

CHAPTER THREE

I was eight and a half when Léonie left
school and I took her place at the abbey. I
was more advanced than any child of my
age, and I was put in a class of older pupils.
One of them was between fourteen and fifteen. She wasn't at all intelligent, but she
knew how to dominate the other pupils and
even the mistresses. Though I was so young,
I was nearly always at the top of the class
and the nuns were very fond of me. So, very
understandably, this girl was jealous of me
and she paid me out in a thousand ways for
my small triumphs. I was so timid and easily
upset that I didn't know how to look after
myself. All I did was to cry and say nothing.
I didn't tell even you about it. I was not
strong enough to rise above it all, and so I
suffered terribly. Fortunately I went home

every evening. There I cheered up, jumped on Daddy's knee, told him the marks I'd been given, and a kiss from him made me forget all my troubles. I was overjoyed when I told him the result of my first examination. I was top of the class and was given a silver badge. As a reward, Daddy gave me a four-sou piece. I put it in my money box, and nearly every Thursday a similar coin joined it. I had a very real need of being given treats like these at home. Without them, my life at school would have been far too hard.

Every Thursday was a half-holiday, but they were not like the holidays you used to give me and which I often used to spend with Daddy in his upstairs room. I loved playing with Céline when we were alone together, but on these Thursdays I had to play with other children. It upset me very much, for I didn't know how to play like them, and so I wasn't a very pleasant companion. I did my best to imitate the others, but never succeeded. What gave me the greatest pleasure was when, at my uncle's, I found myself alone with my cousin Marie, for she let me decide what to play and I used to choose a game very different from the usual ones. We became two hermits, possessing only a little hut, a patch of wheat, and a vegetable garden. We spent our time in ceaseless contemplation: in other words, we took turn and turnabout in prayer and work. Everything was done in silence and with perfect religious decorum. When my aunt took us for a walk, we continued this game in the street. The two hermits said the Rosary, using their fingers as beads so as to be unobserved. One day, though, the youngest hermit had been given a little cake for lunch and she forgot and made a huge sign of the Cross before starting to eat it—which attracted the stares of the worldly passers-by.

Marie and I always held the same opinions and the same tastes, but our desire to behave alike sometimes went too far. Coming home from school one evening, I said to Marie: "You must guide me. I'm going to shut my eyes." "I want to shut mine too," she replied. No sooner said than done. Without another word, we did it. As we were on the pavement, we weren't in danger from carriages, and we went along for a few minutes, enjoying the pleasure of walking without seeing where we were going. But then we bumped into some boxes displaying goods at the door of a shop and knocked them flying. A furious shopkeeper rushed out to rescue his stuff. We scrambled to our feet and ran off as fast as we could with our eyes wide open and listening to the well-deserved scolding of Jeanne, who was just as angry as the shopkeeper.

So far I have said nothing about how close I was to Céline. I should never finish if I told everything. At Lisieux our relationship changed: she had become a little rascal and I had developed into a most quiet child but too much of a crybaby. This difference didn't stop us loving each other more and more. We had little arguments sometimes, but they were never serious and fundamentally we felt and thought the same. Never once has my darling little sister hurt me. She has been like the sunshine, always cheering and comforting me. How bravely she used to stand up for me at school if I was falsely accused of something!

That's the age when one is never bored or jaded, and our fresh young souls expanded like flowers rejoicing in the morning dew. And like flowers we were stirred by the same breezes. The same things made us sad or happy. We shared every joy—a fact driven home to me on that marvellous day when Céline made her first Communion.

As I was only seven, I had not started going to school, but I have the happiest memories of how you prepared her. Every evening she sat on your knee and you told her of the tremendous experience she was going to have. I drank in every word, for I was eager to be prepared myself. But I was often sent away because I was thought to be too young. I was most distressed. I thought four years was not too long to spend preparing to receive God. One evening I heard you tell her that she must begin a new way of life after her first Communion. I instantly decided not to wait till my turn came, but to start this new life when Céline did.

I had never realised how much I loved her as during the three days she spent in retreat before her Communion. I was separated from her for the first time in my life. The day of Céline's first Communion made as great an impression on me as my own did. When I woke in the morning, I felt overwhelmed with joy. "It's today! The great day has come!" I kept saying this over and over again. It seemed as if I were going to make my first Communion, and I believe that I received so many graces that I think of it as one of the most beautiful days of my life.

I have gone back a little to recall this happy memory, but now I have to speak of that grievous separation which almost broke my heart—when Jesus took away from me that little mother whom I loved so dearly. I had once told you that I wanted to be a hermit and go away with you into a far-off desert. You replied that that was what you wanted too, but that you would wait until I was old enough to go. You weren't, of course, being serious, but I took this promise quite seriously and so I was horrified to hear you talking to Marie about your forthcoming entry into Carmel. I didn't know what Carmel was, but I realised that you were leaving me to go into a convent and I knew that you would not wait for me and that I was going to lose my second mother.

How can I express the agony I suffered. In a flash I understood what life was. Until then I had not seen it as too sad a business, but now I saw it as it really was—a thing of suffering and continual partings. I cried bitterly, for I knew nothing then of the joy of sacrifice. I was weak, so weak that I thought it a great grace that I could endure a trial which seemed so much beyond my strength.

I shall never forget how tenderly you comforted me. You explained what life in Carmel was like and it seemed wonderful. When I was thinking about what you had told me, I felt that Carmel was the desert where God wanted me to hide myself too. This feeling was so strong that I had not the least doubt about it. I was not being swept away by any childish dream. I was certain it was a call from God. I longed to enter Carmel, not because of you, but solely because of Jesus. Many thoughts came to me that I can't put into words, but they filled my heart with peace.

Next day I told you of my longing and you saw it as the will of God. You told me that before long I could go with you to see the prioress of Carmel and that I must tell her about God's promptings. A Sunday was the day chosen for this solemn visit, but I was most embarrassed when I learned that my cousin Marie was to go with me and stay with me. As it was essential that I should be able to talk in private, I had to think of something. And so I told Marie that the privilege of visiting the prioress meant that we must be very polite and on our best behaviour. To do that we should have to tell her our inmost thoughts, so we should have to leave each other alone in the parlour for a short time. Marie did not relish having to tell secrets she had not got, but she did what I said, and so I was able to be alone with the prioress. When she had heard what I had to say, Mother Marie of Gonzaga believed that I had a vocation, but she told me that nine-year-old postulants were not received and that I should have to wait until I was sixteen. I resigned myself to this, in spite of my intense longing to enter Carmel as soon as possible and to make my first Communion when you took the veil.

The second of October arrived at last, a day of tears and blessings when Jesus plucked the first of his flowers, she who was to be the mother of those who joined her a few years later. I can still see the spot where I had my last kiss from you. My aunt took us all to Mass, whilst Daddy ascended Mount Carmel to offer his first sacrifice. We wept so much as we went into church that everyone looked at us in astonishment, but I didn't care and their looks didn't stop my tears.

Perhaps you think I am exaggerating a little what I suffered. I am well aware that I should not have been so upset, as I hoped to follow you into Carmel, but my soul was very immature and I had to suffer a great deal before I entered Carmel.

The second of October was the day when I was due to go back to school, and I had to go in spite of my unhappiness. In the afternoon my aunt came and accompanied us to Carmel and I saw you, my darling Pauline, behind the grille. What I suffered during that first meeting! I swear that all the distress I endured before your entry was nothing in comparison with the anguish I suffered afterwards. Every Thursday we all visited Carmel. I had been used to talking to you freely and frankly, and now it was with great difficulty that I could snatch two or three minutes with you at the end of the half-hour we were allowed in the parlour. It's hardly surprising that I spent them in tears and went away heartbroken. I didn't realise that it was out of politeness to my aunt that you spoke more to Jeanne and Marie than to Céline and me. And as I didn't understand this, I cried from the bottom of my heart: "I've lost Pauline!" My character was developed at such an astonishing rate by this suffering that it was not long before I became ill.

My illness was undoubtedly caused by the devil. He was enraged by your becoming a Carmelite, and he wished to punish me for the harm our family was to do him in the future. But he did not know that the Queen of Heaven watched over her frail little flower,

that, from her throne, she smiled down on her, and that she quelled
the storm just when her flower might have been broken beyond
recovery.

Towards the end of the year I started to have a continual
headache. But as it was not very violent and I could carry on with
my schoolwork, no one worried about it. It lasted until Easter, 1883.
Daddy went to Paris with Marie and Léonie, and Céline and I
stayed with my aunt. When I was alone one evening with my uncle,
he began speaking to me about Mummy and the past. He spoke so
kindly that I was deeply moved and began to sob. He said that I was
too sentimental and needed taking out of myself. After talking it
over with my aunt, he decided that I must be kept thoroughly entertained during the Easter holidays. That same evening I fell ill.
Everyone was upset and my aunt had to keep me at her place. She
looked after me as if she had been my mother. When Daddy and
my sisters arrived back from Paris, they were in great distress when
they heard the news. Father thought I should go insane or die, yet
he showed wonderful resignation. And so did Marie. By such resignation God was glorified. Marie suffered greatly because of me,
and I am immensely grateful for all the care she showered on me.
Her heart told her what I needed, and a mother's heart is far wiser
than a doctor's: it can guess what is best for her sick child. Marie
had to come and stay at my uncle's, for I wasn't fit to be taken
home.

The day drew near when you, Pauline, were to take the veil.
Everyone avoided speaking about it in front of me, for they knew
how upset I was at the prospect of not being there. But I often
spoke about it and said I should be well enough to go and see my
darling Pauline. And, indeed, God did not mean to withhold this
consolation from me, or, rather, He wanted to comfort His spouse
who had suffered so greatly because of her little sister's illness. And

so I was able to hug my darling mother, to sit on her knee and shower her with caresses. She looked lovely in her white raiment. It was a lovely day to have in the midst of my suffering, but a day soon ends. Soon I had to step into the carriage which bore me far away from Pauline. I was put to bed as soon as we arrived at Les Buissonnets, although I declared I was quite better and needed no more attention. Alas! I was only at the start of my trial! Next day I had a sharp relapse, and my illness took such a serious turn that, humanly speaking, it seemed I should never recover.

I don't know how to describe this illness, it was so strange. I said and did things unrelated to what I was thinking. Most of the time I seemed delirious and came out with senseless phrases, yet I am certain that I never lost my reason for a single second. Sometimes I was completely exhausted and lay quite motionless. Then I would have let anyone do what they wished with me—even kill me. Yet I heard all that was said and I still remember it. For a long time I could not open my eyes except for a moment when I was alone. I believe the devil was given physical power over me, but that he could not touch my soul or mind—except to fill me with terrible fears of certain things. For example, I was terrified of some very ordinary remedies that they tried in vain to make me take. Yet if God allowed the devil to approach me, He also sent me angels of flesh and blood. Marie never left me, looking after me and comforting me with a mother's tenderness. She never lost her patience in spite of all the trouble I gave her, for I never wanted her to go out of the room. When she went to take her meals with Daddy, I never stopped calling for her all the time she was away, and Victoire, who stayed with me, had sometimes to go and fetch her. I made no complaint, though, when Marie went to Mass or to see you.

My uncle and aunt were just as good to me. My dear aunt came to see me every day and brought me scores of little presents. I cannot describe how my love for my uncle and aunt deepened at that time. I realised more clearly than ever the meaning of the words Father so often used about them: "They are not like ordinary relatives." Later his own experience showed him he was not mistaken, and now he must watch over and bless those who looked after him with such loving care.

Léonie and darling Céline—is there anything they didn't do for their Thérèse? Instead of going for a walk on Sundays, they spent most of the day shut up with a wretched little girl who was almost like an idiot. Oh, my darling sisters, what suffering I caused you! No one has caused you so much trouble as I have, and no one has received as much love as you have poured out on me. Fortunately heaven is there to help me. My Spouse is very rich and I shall use the treasures of His love to repay a hundredfold all that you have suffered because of me.

It was the lovely month of May, when all nature is gay and decked with flowers; only the *Little Flower* drooped and seemed as if blighted for ever. Yet the sun was near to her—the sun of the miraculous statue of the Blessed Virgin, that statue which had spoken twice to Mummy. Often, very often, the Little Flower turned towards this blessed sun.

One day I saw Daddy come into Marie's room where I was lying. He looked very sad and gave her some gold coins and told her to write to Paris for Masses for my recovery to be said at the church of Our Lady of Victories. How touched I was to see the love and faith of my beloved King! I longed to be able to tell him that I was cured, but I had raised his hopes too often already. Besides, my longings couldn't perform a miracle and a miracle was needed to cure me. Yes, it was a miracle that was needed and it was Our Lady of Victories who performed it.

On the Sunday, during the novena for me in Paris, Marie went into the garden and left me with Léonie who was sitting reading near the window. After a minute or two I began calling, almost in a whisper: "Marie, Marie!" Léonie took no notice, as she was so used to my doing this. Before long I raised my voice and Marie came in. I saw her quite clearly, but I did not recognise her and went on shouting: "Marie! Marie!" I was suffering intensely and Marie suffered even more. She tried in vain to make me recognise her. Then, with Léonie and Céline, she knelt by my bed. They gazed towards the statue of the Blessed Virgin and prayed to her with all the passion of a mother asking for the life of her child. Marie got her desire. I could find no help on earth, so I also turned to my heavenly Mother and beseeched her to have pity on me. Suddenly the Blessed Virgin glowed with a beauty beyond anything I had ever seen. Her face was alive with kindness and an infinite tenderness, but it was her enchanting smile which really moved me to the depths. My pain vanished and two great tears crept down my cheeks—tears of pure joy. "Oh," I thought, "how happy I am that the Blessed Virgin has smiled at me. But I will never tell anyone about it, for if I do my happiness will be lost."

I looked at Marie, who was gazing lovingly at me and seemed moved as if she guessed the favour granted me by the Blessed Virgin. It was indeed to her and her prayers that I owed the grace of a smile from the Queen of Heaven. When she saw me staring at the statue, she said to herself: "Thérèse is cured!" She was right. The Little Flower had come back to life. And the sun which had warmed her did not stop there. Sweetly and gently the Little Flower was strengthened, so that five years later she blossomed on the fertile slopes of Carmel.

As I've said, Marie guessed that the Blessed Virgin had given me a grace, so, when I was alone with her, she asked me what I had seen. I could not hold out against her tender, insistent questioning. I was so astonished to see my secret known without my having said a word that I told her everything. Alas, as I had feared, my joy changed to grief. For four years, the memory of this great grace caused me real spiritual anguish. I regained my happiness only at the feet of Our Lady of Victories. There it was restored to me in all its fulness. I shall tell of this second favour later. Now I must tell you how my joy changed to sorrow. After Marie had heard my simple, straightforward story of this grace, she asked me if she could tell it to Carmel. I could not say no. On my first visit to Carmel after my illness, I was overjoyed at seeing you in the habit of the Blessed Virgin. It was a wonderfully happy moment for us both. There was so much to talk about, but my heart was so full that I could say hardly a word. Mother Marie of Gonzaga was present and she treated me most affectionately. I met some of the other nuns and they questioned me about the grace I had received. Some wanted to know if the Blessed Virgin was carrying the Child Jesus, and others asked if there was a great blaze of light. All these questions disturbed me and made me wretched. I could only say: "The Blessed Virgin looked most lovely and I saw her smile at me." Only her face had moved me, but I saw that the nuns imagined something quite different and I thought that perhaps I had lied. If only I had kept my secret, I should have kept my happiness as well, but the Blessed Virgin let me suffer for the good of my soul. Otherwise, I might have become vain. As it was, I suffered such humiliation that I could regard myself only with deep contempt. Only in heaven shall I be able to tell what I suffered.

CHAPTER FOUR

Telling of that visit to Carmel reminds me of the first I paid after Pauline's entry. On the morning of that day I thought of what name I should have in Carmel. I knew there was a Sister Thérèse of Jesus, but I was determined that my own lovely name of Thérèse should not be taken from me. Suddenly I though of the little Jesus to whom I was so devoted and I exclaimed: "How happy I should be to be called Thérèse of the Child Jesus!" During my visit I said nothing of this thought of mine, but the prioress asked the nuns what name I should be given and the name I had chosen came to them. I was overjoyed. That we should all have thought of this name seemed to show the graciousness of my beloved little Jesus.

So far I've said nothing about my love of

books and pictures. And yet, darling Mother, it is to the lovely pictures you showed me that I owe some of my greatest happiness and the strongest incentives to goodness. I lost all sense of time as I looked at them. The one, for example, called "The Little Flower of the Divine Prisoner" held such meaning for me that I entered into a kind of ecstasy and I offered myself to Jesus as His little flower.

As I was no good at games, I would have been happy to spend all my time reading. Fortunately I was guided in my reading and given books which entertained me and also strengthened my mind and character. The time allowed me for reading was strictly limited, which gave me the chance of mortifying myself, because the instant the allotted time ended, I broke off at once, even in the middle of the most interesting paragraph. This love of reading lasted till I entered Carmel. I read innumerable books, but God never allowed me to read one which might have harmed me. I read some tales of chivalry, but it wasn't long before God made me realise that the true glory is that which is eternal and that, to achieve it, there is no need to perform outstanding deeds. Instead, one must remain hidden and perform one's good deeds so that the right hand knows not what the left hand does. When I read stories about the deeds of the great French heroines—especially of the Venerable Joan of Arc, I longed to imitate them and felt stirred by the same inspiration which moved them. It was then that I received one of the greatest graces of my life, for, at that age, I didn't receive the spiritual enlightenment which now floods my soul. I was made to understand that the glory I was to win would never be seen during my lifetime. My glory would consist in becoming a great saint! This desire might seem presumptuous, seeing how weak and imperfect I was and still am, even after eight years as a nun, yet I always feel the same fearless certainty that I shall become a great saint. I'm not relying on my own merits, as I have none, but I put my hope in Him who is goodness and holiness Himself. It is He alone who, satisfied with my feeble efforts, will raise me to Him, will clothe me with His infinite merits, and will make me a saint. I did not realise then how much one had to suffer to be a saint, but God soon showed me this through those trials I have already written about.

Now I will go on with my story where I left off. Three months after I was cured, Daddy took us on a trip to Alençon. It was the first time I'd been back there and I was overjoyed to see again the places where I'd spent my early childhood. During this visit to Alençon I made what I can call my first appearance in the world. I was surrounded with gaiety and pleasure and was entertained, pampered, and generally made much of. For a fortnight my path was strewn with flowers, and I must confess that this life was not without its attractions for me. How right the Book of Wisdom is when it says: "Such witchery evil has, to tarnish honour." When one is ten, one is easily dazzled, so I think it is a great grace that we left Alençon, as our friends there were too worldly and too clever at mixing the pleasures of the world with the service of God. They scarcely gave a thought to death, and yet death has called many of the people I knew and they were young and rich and happy. I like to think of the charming surroundings in which they lived and to wonder where they themselves are now and of what use to them are their châteaux and their gardens where I saw them enjoying the good things of life. And I knew that all is fleeting that we cherish here under the sun. The only good thing is to love God with all one's heart and to stay poor in spirit.

Perhaps Jesus wished to show me what the world was like, before He paid me His first visit, so that I might choose more willingly the path I should promise Him to follow.

No shadows cloud the memory of the time of my first Communion. I don't think I could have been better disposed: all the troubles which were disturbing my soul vanished for nearly a year. You remember, Mother, the wonderful little book you gave me three months before my first Communion? It made my preparation both quick and thorough. Even though I had been preparing myself for a long time, your book made it plain that my heart must have a new ardour and be filled with fresh flowers so that Jesus could delight in resting there. Every day I made many sacrifices and prayed and thought continually of God. Marie replaced you, and I used to sit on her knee drinking in all she told me. I think that all the warmth and greatness of her soul entered mine. Just as the warriors of old taught their children the art of war, so she instructed me in the battle of life and spoke of the victor's palm. She told me too of that eternal treasure of which one can gather some each day, and of the folly of passing it by when one has only to stretch out a hand to take it. She showed me how one could achieve sanctity by being faithful in the smallest matters. How eloquent she was! I wished others could have been there and heard the wisdom of her instruction. I was so moved by it that, in my simplicity, I believed the greatest sinners would have been just as moved and would abandon their earthly wealth and seek only to gain that of heaven.

No one had yet taught me how to practise mental prayer, though I longed to. Marie, though, thought I was devout enough and would allow me only to say my prayers. At school one day a mistress asked me what I did when I was alone in the holidays. I told her that I used to go into a space there was behind my bed which I could shut off with the bed curtain. And there I used to think. "But what do you think about?" she asked. "I think about God, about life . . . about eternity. Well, I just think!" She laughed at this, and long afterwards she loved to remind me of the time when I thought, and she would ask me if I still thought. I realise now that I was engaged in mental prayer without knowing it and that God was teaching me it in secret.

The three months of preparation went quickly, and then I had to enter retreat at school and stay there at night. Though I had often been very unhappy at school, it was all wiped out by the marvellous happiness of those few days spent waiting for Jesus. I am sure one can experience such joy only in a religious community. Where there are only a few children, it is easy to give each one individual attention and certainly the nuns were like mothers to us. I got even more attention than the rest of us. Every night as the headmistress was going her rounds with her little lamp, she would come to my bed and give me a kiss. I was so touched by the kindness she always showed me that I told her I was going to entrust her with a secret. I drew my precious little book from under the pillow and showed it to her with my eyes shining with joy.

I listened most attentively to Father Domin's instruction and made careful notes. But I didn't put down any of my thoughts, as I knew I should not forget them. It was with great delight that I went with the nuns to every office. I stood out from my companions because of a large crucifix Léonie had given me. I pushed it into my belt like a missionary, and everyone thought it was to imitate my Carmelite sister. It was true that my thoughts were with you. I knew you also were in retreat—not in preparation for Jesus giving Himself to you, but for you to give yourself to Him.

At last the most wonderful of all days arrived. Every little detail of those heavenly hours is with me still. I remember how joyfully we woke at dawn, the grave and tender kisses of the nuns, the dressing room where we were all clothed, and, above all, our entering the chapel and singing the morning hymn:

"O blessed altar, ringed with angels."

But I am not going to give every detail. Some things lose their fragrance when opened to the air, and there are stirrings of the soul which cannot be put into words without destroying their delicacy.

Oh, how sweet the first kiss of Jesus was! It was a kiss of love. I knew that I was loved and I declared: "I love You and I give myself to You for ever!" Jesus made no demand on me; He asked for no sacrifices. For a long time Jesus and little Thérèse had gazed at each other and they understood each other. On that day it was no longer a matter of gazing: it was a union. There were no longer two of us. Thérèse had disappeared like a drop of water lost in the depth of the ocean. Only Jesus remained—as Master and King. For had not Thérèse begged Him to take away her freedom? Freedom frightened her, for she knew herself to be so weak and feeble that she wished to be united with the divine Power for ever.

Her joy was too great, too deep to be contained. She wept. Her companions were amazed and afterwards they said: "Why on earth did she cry? Something must have been upsetting her. Perhaps it was because her mother wasn't there, nor her Carmelite sister she loves so much." They couldn't understand that such a flood of divine joy cannot be borne without tears. How could my mother's absence hurt me on the day of my first Communion? Heaven dwelt in my soul and Mummy had been there for a long time, and when Jesus visited me so did my beloved mother. She blessed me as she rejoiced at my happiness. Nor did I weep at your absence. On that day nothing but joy filled my heart, and I united myself with you who were giving yourself for ever to Him who gave Himself so lovingly to me.

In the afternoon I recited the Act of Consecration to the Blessed Virgin. It was very fitting for me to speak in the name of my companions to my heavenly Mother, as I had lost my earthly mother so soon. I pledged myself to her with all my heart, like a child flinging itself into the arms of its mother and begging her to protect it. It seemed that she looked down on her little flower and smiled, for had she not healed me with a smile I had *seen?* Had she not placed her Jesus within the petals of her little flower?

In the evening of this wonderful day Daddy walked hand in hand with me to Carmel, and there I saw you, Pauline, become the bride of Jesus, with your veil, white like mine, and your crown of roses. There was no trace of sadness in my joy, for I hoped to join you soon and wait for heaven at your side. I enjoyed the celebrations at home that evening and I was delighted with the lovely watch my King gave me, but it was a calm happiness I felt and nothing disturbed my inner peace. Night at last ended this lovely day, for even the brightest day finishes with the dark: only one day will be without end—that of our first and everlasting Communion in heaven.

The next day was lovely too but tinged with sadness. The pretty dress Marie had bought me and all my presents did not satisfy me. Henceforth only Jesus could do that, and I longed for the time when I could receive Him again. I was allowed to on Ascension Day and I knew the joy of kneeling before the altar between Daddy and Marie. Once again I wept and I said over and over again the words of St. Paul: "I am alive; or rather, not I; it is Christ that lives in me." After this Communion my longing to receive God grew and grew, and I was allowed to go on all the main feasts. Marie took me on her knees on the evening before these days and prepared me just as she had done for my first Communion. I recall how she once spoke to me about suffering. She said she thought God would always carry me like a baby rather than make me tread the path of suffering. After Holy Communion next day I remembered this and I was seized with a passionate longing to suffer. I felt absolutely certain that Jesus had many, many crosses in store for me. My soul was flooded with such consolation that I regard it as one of the greatest graces of my life. I was drawn to suffering. It had about it a charm which delighted me, though I didn't really understand much about this charm, for until then I had suffered without loving suffering. But from that day I felt a deep, true love for it.

I also had another longing: to love only God and to find no joy apart from Him. During my Communion I often repeated these words from *The Imitation of Christ:* "O God, who art unutterable sweetness, turn to bitterness for me all the comforts of earth!" The words came effortlessly from my lips. I said them like a child reciting words put into its mind by a beloved friend. I shall tell you later how Our Lord deigned to fulfil my longing and how He and He alone was my treasure and delight. If I told you about it now, I should have to jump ahead to my life as a young girl and I've still got to tell you a lot more about me as a child.

Not long after my first Communion, I went into retreat again for my Confirmation and prepared with great care for the descent of the Holy Ghost. I couldn't understand there being any lack of preparedness for this Sacrament of love. Usually there's only one day of retreat before Confirmation, but as the bishop was unable to come on the appointed day, I was able to spend two days in retreat. How happy I was! Like the apostles, I awaited with joy the coming of the Holy Ghost. I rejoiced that I should soon be a full Christian, with my forehead marked for ever with the mystic cross drawn there by the bishop as he administers this Sacrament.

The moment came at last. I felt no rushing wind when the Holy Ghost descended, but, instead, that gentle breeze whose murmur Elias heard on Horeb. And on that day I acquired the strength to suffer. The martyrdom of my soul was soon to start.

After these wonderful, unforgettable days my life slipped back into its ordinary routine. I had to resume my school life which I found so unpleasant. At the time of my first Communion I loved being with children of my own age, all of them full of good intentions and all of them, like me, determined to strive hard to be good. Now I went back among a very different type, undisciplined and naughty. It upset me very much. I was cheerful enough, but I didn't know how to play games, and so during playtime I often used to stand by a tree and think of serious matters. I invented a game which pleased me: I used to bury the poor little birds we found lying dead under the trees. Many of the girls helped me, and our cemetery became very pretty, for we planted it with tiny shrubs and plants. I also liked telling stories which I made up and then I got quite a crowd round me, including some of the big girls. The same story would continue for several days, for I liked to make it more and more exciting as I saw, from the faces of my audience, what kind of impression it was making. But the nuns soon stopped my storytelling, as they wanted to see us exercise our bodies rather than our tongues.

I easily understood my lessons but I found it hard to learn anything by heart, yet I was always first in catechism. Our chaplain was very satisfied with me and called me his "little doctor" because my name was Thérèse.

I tried to make friends with the girls at school who were of my own age, particularly with two of them. I really loved them and they loved me as far as they were capable of true love. But how small and feeble the human heart is! It wasn't long before I saw that they just didn't understand my kind of love. One of these girls had to go and stay with her family for some months. I thought about her all the time she was away and cherished a little ring she had given me. I was overjoyed when she came back, but she was quite cool towards me. She didn't understand how I loved her. I was upset, but I didn't beg for an unwilling affection. Yet God has made me so that when once I love I love for ever, and so I continue to pray for this girl and I love her still. When I saw how Céline loved one of the nuns, I tried to imitate her, but I didn't succeed, as I didn't know how to get into people's good graces. It was a fortunate ignorance which has saved me from much evil. I am profoundly grateful to Jesus who has never let me find anything but bitterness in earthly friendships. With a nature like mine, I should have been trapped and had my wings clipped and then how should I have "flown away and found rest"? It's impossible for one bound by human affection to have intimate union with God. I've seen so many souls, dazzled by this deluding light, fly into it and burn their wings like silly moths. Then they turn again to the true unfading light of love and, with new and more splendid wings, fly to Jesus, that divine Fire which burns yet does not destroy. I know that Jesus considered me too weak to be exposed to temptation. If I had seen this false light shining before me, I should have been wholly destroyed. I've been saved from that. I have found nothing but bitterness where stronger souls have found happiness and yet remained properly detached. So it's no merit on my part that I never became entangled by love of creatures; I was saved only by the great mercy of God. I am aware that without Him I should have fallen as low as St. Magdalene and the words Our Lord said to Simon the Pharisee filled my soul with sweetness: "He loves little, who has little forgiven him." I know that is true, but I also know that Jesus has forgiven me more than He did St. Magdalene. If only I could explain what I feel! But here's an illustration which may make my thoughts a little clearer. Suppose the son of a clever doctor falls over a stone in the road and breaks his leg. His father rushes to the spot and, with loving care, uses every ounce of his skill to heal him. His son is soon healed and is grateful. There's no doubt the boy is quite right to love such a father. But now let us suppose that the father learns that a dangerous stone lies in the road, goes there before his son, and, unseen by anyone, takes away the stone. Now the boy, who knows nothing of the mishap he has been spared by his father's loving foresight, will show him no particular gratitude and will love him less than if he had been healed by him. Yet if the boy knew the danger he had escaped, would he not love his father more? Well, now, I am that child, protected by the foreseeing love of a Father who sent His Son "to call sinners, not the just." He wants me to love Him because He has forgiven me not just a great deal, but everything. Without waiting for me to love Him with a great love like St. Magdalene, He has made me understand that He loved me first with a full, all-seeing love, so now I adore Him even unto folly. I have heard it said that a pure soul does not love with the passion of one that has sinned but repented. What a lie that is!

I've wandered a long way from my subject, so I hasten back to it. The terrible disease of scruples attacked me when I was in retreat for my second Communion. One cannot really understand this torture unless one has suffered it. It's quite impossible to tell what I suffered for eighteen months. Even the simplest of my thoughts and acts became a source of worry. I found peace only when I told Marie everything, and that wasn't easy to do, for I felt I had to tell her my most fantastic imaginings. After I had unburdened myself, I felt a moment's peace, but it went in a flash and my torment began all over again. What patience Marie must have had to listen to me without ever showing a trace of boredom! I fell ill again, and so I left school when I was thirteen and had private lessons several times a week with Madame Papineau. She was a very good and well-educated woman who lived with her mother. Quite apart from what I learnt, these lessons were useful because they made me know the world—which sounds surprising, I know. Sitting in that room full of old-fashioned furniture, I saw all kinds of visitors—priests, ladies, young girls, and others. Madame Papineau's mother used to do most of the talking so as to leave her daughter free to go on teaching me, but I didn't learn much when visitors were there. For though I kept my nose in my book, I heard all that was said, though it might have been better if I hadn't. One woman would say what lovely hair I had and another, thinking that I couldn't hear her, would ask as she left who was the young girl who was so pretty. These remarks, which were all the more flattering as I was not supposed to hear them, gave me enough pleasure to show me clearly how full of self-love I was. How I pity people who lose their souls! It's so easy to go astray along the world's primrose paths. Of course, for even a slightly enlightened soul, the world's sweetness is mixed with bitterness, and a moment's flattery cannot fill the immense gulf of such a soul's desires. But what should I have become if my heart had not been drawn towards God from its first awakening and if the world had smiled on me from my birth? O beloved Mother, how gratefully do I sing of the mercies of the Lord! To quote the Book of Wisdom, has He not "caught me away, before wickedness could pervert my thoughts, before wrongdoing could allure my heart"? The Blessed Virgin also watched over her little flower. She took her up into her own mountain before she opened into full flower. As I waited for this, my love deepened for my heavenly Mother. To prove how much I loved her, I did something which needed a lot of doing. I'll tell you about it. Almost as soon as I started school, I was received into the Association of the Holy Angels. I loved the devotional practices this meant, for I took special delight in praying to the angels and particularly to him given me by God to be my companion during my exile on earth. Not long after my first Communion the ribbon for candidates seeking to become Children of Mary replaced that of the Holy Angels. As I had left school before finishing my studies, I was not allowed to be a candidate. I confess this didn't at first worry me, but then I thought that all my sisters had been Children of Mary and I was afraid of being not so fully a child of my heavenly Mother as they were. So I went back to school and pleaded very humbly—which I didn't like doing at all—to be received as a candidate. The headmistress didn't want to refuse, but she made it a condition that I should return to school two afternoons a week so that it could be seen if I was worthy of being a Child of Mary. This horrified me. Some of the other girls, former pupils like me, had friends among the nuns with whom they could spend these afternoons. But I hadn't. I sat and worked in silence at my sewing and then, when I had finished, as no one took any notice of me, I went to the chapel and climbed up into the tribune. There I remained before the Blessed Sacrament until Daddy came to take me home. There I found my sole comfort: Jesus, my only friend. I could talk only to Him. Talking to other people bored me, even when we spoke about religion. I felt it better to speak to God than about Him. There's often so much self-love involved in chatter about spiritual things! I went back to school only for the Blessed Virgin. Sometimes I felt lonely, very lonely, but then peace and courage would come back to me if I repeated the line:

"The world's thy ship and not thy home."

These words cheered me when I was very young, and now, in spite of the years which have wiped away so many memories of childish piety, the image of a ship always charms me and helps me to endure my exile. The Book of Wisdom also says: "The ship that ploughs angry waves, what trace is left of her passage?"

When I think of these things, my mind plunges into the infinite and I seem to stand already on the shore of heaven and to be embraced by Jesus. The Virgin Mary comes to meet me, accompanied by Daddy and Mummy and those four little angels, my brothers and sisters. I seem to enjoy already that family life which never ends.

But before being reunited with my family in our heavenly Father's house, I had still to suffer many earthly partings. In the year when I became a Child of Mary, Our Lady took Marie from me—Marie, my sole support, my guide and comforter. Marie knew everything that went on in my soul. She knew too of my longing for Carmel. I loved her so much that I could not have lived without her.

Every year my aunt invited us to go and stay with her at Trouville. But she asked us one at a time, and I always wanted to go with Marie. I was very unhappy when I couldn't. But once I enjoyed Trouville. It was the year Daddy went to Constantinople. We were very upset at the thought of Daddy being so far away, so to distract us a little Marie sent Céline and me to spend a fortnight by the sea. I enjoyed myself thoroughly because Céline was with me. My aunt provided every kind of amusement for us—donkey rides, fishing, etc. Though I was twelve and a half, I was still very young, and I remember how delighted I was at wearing some sky-blue ribbon my aunt gave me for my hair. I remember too confessing this at Trouville, for even this childish pleasure seemed a sin to me.

One evening something happened which astonished me. My cousin, Marie, who never had really good health, spent a lot of her time crying and complaining. My aunt used to soothe her and talk most tenderly to her, but Marie would continue to cry and say how her head ached. I also had a headache nearly every day, but I hadn't complained about it. But now I decided to imitate Marie. So I sat in an armchair in a corner of the sitting room and began to cry. At once Jeanne and my aunt came to ask what was the matter with me. Like Marie, I said: "I've a headache." But I just could not make them believe that I cried because of a headache. Instead of fussing over me, they spoke to me as if I were grown-up, and Jeanne reproached me for not being frank with my aunt. She thought my conscience was troubled about something. So I was taught my lesson and made up my mind never to imitate anyone else. I understood the fable of the donkey and the dog. I was the donkey who saw how the dog was praised and patted and so put his great hoof on the table so that he could have his share of attention. Unlike the poor donkey, I wasn't beaten, but I was taught a lesson which cured me for good of wanting to draw attention to myself.

Next year, which was the year Marie left us, my aunt invited me to Trouville again—but alone this time, and, after two or three days I was so homesick that I fell ill and had to be taken back to Lisieux. The moment I reached home I was cured. And this was the child from whom God was going to snatch the only support of her life!

After Marie entered Carmel, I was still beset with scruples, but, as I could no longer tell her about them, I turned to heaven. I spoke to the four little angels who had gone there ahead of me, for I thought that as they had never known either grief or fear, they would be sure to have pity on their poor little sister suffering on earth. With childlike simplicity I told them that, as I was the youngest of the family, I had always been the most tenderly loved by my sisters and that if they themselves had remained on earth they would have given me a similar love. That they were in heaven seemed no reason why they should forget me. On the contrary: they could draw on the divine treasury and obtain peace for me from it and thus show me that in heaven one still knew how to love! I hadn't to wait long for an answer. Waves of delicious peace soon flooded my soul and I knew that I was loved in heaven as well as on earth. From that moment my love for my little brothers and sisters in heaven grew, and I loved to talk with them about the sorrows of exile and of my longing to join them soon in heaven.

CHAPTER FIVE

I did not deserve the graces heaven showered
on me. I had many faults. It's true that I
longed to be good, but I had an odd way of
going about it. As I was the youngest, I
wasn't used to looking after myself. Céline
tidied our bedroom and I never did a stroke
of housework. But after Marie entered
Carmel, I sometimes used to make our
beds—to please God. Sometimes, too, when
Céline was away, I looked after her plants.
As I did this for no other reason than to
please God, I shouldn't have expected any
thanks for it. Yet if Céline didn't look surprised and pleased, I cried with disappoint-
ment.

My extreme sensitiveness made me quite
unendurable. If I ever offended anyone accidentally, instead of making the best of it I

wept bitterly and so made things worse. Then, when I'd stopped weeping, I'd start all over again and weep for having wept. No amount of reasoning with me did me any good and I couldn't cure myself of this wretched fault. I don't know how I dreamt of entering Carmel while I behaved as childishly as this. It needed God to perform a small miracle to make me grown-up in a second, and this miracle He performed on Christmas Day. Jesus, the Child then only an hour old, flooded the darkness of my soul with torrents of light. By becoming weak and frail for me, He gave me strength and courage. He clothed me with His weapons, and from that blessed night I was unconquerable. I went from victory to victory and began to run as a giant. My tears dried up and from then I cried neither often nor easily, thus fulfilling what used to be said to me: "You are crying so much now that later you'll have no tears left."

It was on December 25, 1886, that I received the grace of emerging from childhood—the grace of my complete conversion. We went to midnight Mass where I had the joy of receiving almighty God. When we got home again, I was excited at the thought of my shoes standing, full of presents, in the fireplace. When we were small children, this old custom gave us such delight that Céline wanted to continue treating me like a baby as I was the youngest in the family. Daddy used to love to see my happiness and hear my cries of joy as I pulled out each surprise from the magic shoes, and the delight of my beloved King increased my own. But as Jesus wanted to free me from the faults of childhood, He also took away its innocent pleasures. He arranged matters so that Daddy was irritated at seeing my shoes in the fireplace and spoke about them in a way which hurt me very much: "Thank goodness it's the last time we shall have this kind of thing!" I went upstairs to take off my hat. Céline knew how sensitive I was. She said: "Thérèse, don't go downstairs again. Taking the presents out of your shoes will upset you too much." But Thérèse was not the same girl. Jesus had changed her. I suppressed my tears, ran downstairs, and picked up my shoes. I pulled out my presents with an air of great cheerfulness. Daddy laughed and Céline thought she was dreaming! But it was no dream. Thérèse had got back for good the strength of soul which she had lost when she was four and a half. On this glorious night the third period of my life began. It has been the loveliest of them all and the one richest with heavenly graces. Jesus, satisfied with my goodwill, accomplished in an instant what I had been unable to do in ten years. Like the apostles, we could say: "Master, I have toiled all the night, and caught nothing." Jesus was more merciful to me than to His disciples. He Himself took the net, cast it, and drew it up full of fishes. He made me a fisher of men. I longed to work for the conversion of sinners with a passion I'd never felt before. Love filled my heart, I forgot myself and henceforth I was happy.

One Sunday when I was looking at a picture of Our Lord on the Cross, I saw the Blood coming from one of His hands, and I felt terribly sad to think that It was falling to the earth and that no one was rushing forward to catch It. I determined to stay continually at the foot of the Cross and receive It. I knew that I should then have to spread It among other souls. The cry of Jesus on the Cross—"I am thirsty"—rang continually in my heart and set me burning with a new, intense longing. I wanted to quench the thirst of my Well-Beloved and I myself was consumed with a thirst for souls. I was concerned not with the souls of priests but with those of great sinners which I wanted to snatch from the flames of hell.

God showed me He was pleased with these longings of mine. I'd heard of a criminal who had just been condemned to death for some frightful murders. It seemed that he would die without repenting. I was determined at all costs to save him from hell. I used every means I could. I knew that by myself I could do nothing, so I offered God the infinite merits of Our Lord and the treasures of the Church. I was quite certain that my prayers would be answered, but to give me courage to go on praying for sinners I said to God: "I am sure You will forgive this wretched Pranzini. I shall believe You have done so even if he does not confess or give any other sign of repentance, for I have complete faith in the infinite mercy of Jesus. But I ask You for just one sign of his repentance to encourage me."

This prayer was answered. Daddy never allowed us to read any newspapers, but I thought I was justified in looking at the stories about Pranzini. On the day after his execution I eagerly opened *La Croix* and I had to rush away to hide my tears at what I read. Pranzini had mounted the scaffold without confessing and was ready to thrust his head beneath the guillotine's blade when he suddenly turned, seized the crucifix offered him by the priest, and thrice kissed the Sacred Wounds.

I had been given my sign, and it was typical of the graces Jesus has given me to make me eager to pray for sinners. It was at the sight of the Precious Blood flowing from the Wounds of Jesus that my thirst for souls had been born. I wanted to let them drink of this Immaculate Blood to cleanse them of their sins and the lips of my "first child" had pressed against the Sacred Wounds! What a wonderful reply to my prayers! After this striking favour my longing for souls grew greater every day. I seemed to hear Jesus say to me what He said to the Samaritan Woman: "Give me to drink." It was a real exchange of love: I gave souls the Blood of Jesus and offered Him these purified souls that His thirst might be quenched. The more I gave Him to drink, the more the thirst of my own poor soul increased, and He gave me this burning thirst to show His love for me.

In a short time God had lifted me out of the narrow circle in which I'd been going round and round, quite unable to escape from it. When I see the road He has made me tread, I am profoundly grateful, but it was essential that I should be fit for it, and though I'd made the first and greatest step along it, there still remained much for me to do. Now I was rid of my scruples and my excessive sensitiveness, my mind began to develop. All that was great and lovely had always appealed to me, but now I was gripped by an intense desire for learning. I wasn't satisfied with the lessons of Madame Papineau. I began working on my own at history and science. Other subjects didn't attract me at all, but I loved these two and I learnt more in a few months than in all the years before.

I was at the most dangerous time of life for young girls, but God did for me what Ezechiel recounts: Passing by me, Jesus saw that I was ripe for love. He plighted His troth to me and I became His. He threw His cloak about me, washed me with water and anointed me with oil, clothed me in fine linen and silk, and decked me with bracelets and priceless gems. He fed me on wheat and honey and oil and I had matchless beauty and He made me a great queen. Jesus did all that for me. I could go over every word of what I've just written and show how they applied to me, but the graces I've spoken about before are proof enough. All I'm going to write of now is the food Our Lord gave me so abundantly. For a long time I'd been fed on the wheat of *The Imitation*. It was the only book which did me any good, as I hadn't discovered the treasures of the Gospels. I knew every chapter by heart. I was never without this little book. My aunt often used to open it at random and I would recite whatever chapter appeared. When I was fourteen and had this passion for learning, God added honey and oil to the wheat of *The Imitation*. I found this honey and oil in Father Arminjon's book, *The End of this World and the Mysteries of the Future Life*. Reading it was one of the greatest graces I've known. All the great truths of religion and the secrets of eternity were there and filled my soul with a happiness not of this world. I saw already what God has in store for those who love Him. When I realised how trifling are the sacrifices of this life compared with the rewards of heaven, I wanted to love Jesus, to love Him passinately, and to give Him a thousand tokens of my love whilst I still could.

Céline shared my intimate thoughts. Since Christmas we understood each other perfectly. As Jesus wanted us to go forward together, He united us with bonds stronger than those of blood. He made us sisters in spirit, and we fulfilled those words of our Father, St. John of the Cross: "The young girls run gaily along the path in the track of Your footsteps. The touch of the spark and the spiced wine gives them longings for the Divine." We did indeed follow gaily in the footsteps of Jesus. The sparks of love He cast so generously into our souls and the strong, sweet wine He made us drink swept all the transient things of earth from our gaze and we breathed out words of love inspired by Him.

What wonderful talks we had every evening in our upstairs room! As we gazed out we saw the moon rise slowly above the trees and its silvery light pour over the sleeping world. The stars glittered in the dark blue of the sky and here and there a cloud drifted along blown by the night breeze. Everything drew our souls upwards to heaven. I think we were given many graces. As *The Imitation* says, God sometimes reveals Himself "in great light" or "appears veiled under signs and figures," and it was in this way that He disclosed Himself to us. But how light and transparent was the veil which hid Jesus from our eyes! Doubt wasn't possible and faith and hope were no longer needed, for love made us find on earth Him we sought: "When we were alone, He gave us His kiss, and now no one may despise us."

Such tremendous graces had to bear fruit and it was abundant.

To be good became natural and pleasant for us. At first my face often betrayed the struggle I was having, but gradually spontaneous self-sacrifice came easily. Jesus said: "If ever a man is rich, gifts will be made to him, and his riches will abound." For every grace I made good use of, He gave me many more. He gave Himself to me in Holy Communion far oftener than I should have dared to hope. I had made it a rule to go very faithfully to every Communion allowed me by my confessor, but never to ask him to allow me more. In those days I hadn't the daring I have now, or I should have behaved quite differently, for I'm absolutely certain that people must tell their confessors of the longing they have to receive God. For He does not come down from heaven every day to lie in a golden ciborium: He comes to find another heaven which is infinitely dearer to Him—the heaven of our souls, created in His image, the living temples of the adorable Trinity!

Jesus, who saw what I wanted, moved my confessor to allow me to receive Holy Communion several times a week. I never said a word about what was going on in my soul. The path I trod was so bright and straight that I felt I needed no guide but Jesus. I considered spiritual directors were like mirrors which faithfully reflected the light of Jesus into souls, but I thought that God needed no intermediary where I was concerned. He dealt with me direct!

When a gardener takes trouble over fruit he wants to ripen early, it isn't because he wants to leave them hanging on the tree, but because he wants them to appear on a richly appointed table. It was the same reason that made Jesus shower His favours on His little flower. During His days on earth He exclaimed in a transport of joy: "I give thee praise that thou hast hidden all this from the wise and prudent, and revealed it to little children." As He wished to make His mercy evident through me and as I was small and weak, He stooped down to me and secretly taught me the secrets of His love. If scholars who had spent their lives in study had questioned me, I'm sure they'd have been amazed to come across a fourteen-year-old child who understood the secrets of perfection, secrets which all their learning couldn't reveal to them, for one has to be poor in spirit to understand them. As St. John of the Cross says: "I had neither guide nor light, except that which shone within my heart, and that guided me more surely than the midday sun to the place where He who knew me well awaited me." That place was Carmel, but before I could lie in the "shade cool to rest under" I had to go through many trials. Yet the divine call was so urgent that, if necessary, I'd have plunged through flames to follow Jesus.

There was only one person who encouraged my vocation and that was you, my darling Pauline. In your heart mine found a faithful echo. Without you, it is certain I should not have reached the blessed haven you entered five years before. Yes, I was cut off from you for five years and I thought you were lost to me for ever. But when the moment of crisis came, it was you who pointed out to me the road to follow. I needed that comfort, for my visits to Carmel were becoming more and more painful. I couldn't mention my longing to enter there without feeling rebuffed. Marie thought I was too young and did all she could to hinder me, and you yourself tested me by trying to damp down my ardour. So if my vocation hadn't been genuine, it would have been killed at the start, for I met nothing but obstacles the moment I began to respond to the call of Jesus. I didn't want to say anything to Céline about wanting to enter Carmel at so early an age, and that made me most unhappy, as it was so difficult for me to hide anything from her. But this unhappiness didn't last long, for she soon discovered what I was bent on doing. Far from trying to change my mind, she accepted, with admirable courage, the sacrifice God asked from her. She could have complained that, as she also had a vocation, she should have entered Carmel before me. Instead, she was like the martyrs of old who cheerfully gave a farewell embrace to those who went into the arena before them, consoling themselves with the thought that perhaps they were being kept for greater torments. Thus did Céline let her Thérèse go and stayed behind for the glorious but bloody combat for which Jesus had destined her as the chosen of His love! She shared all my trials and suffering just as if they involved her own vocation. So I had nothing to fear from any opposition by her, but I didn't know how I should tell Daddy. How I suffered before plucking up courage to speak! Yet I had to decide, for I was nearly fourteen and a half and Christmas was only six months away and I was determined to enter Carmel at the very time when, the year before, I had been converted.

I chose the Feast of Pentecost to make my great disclosure. Throughout the day I begged the blessed apostles to pray for me and inspire me with the right words to say. Surely they were the ones to help the timid child God was to make the apostle of apostles by her prayers and sacrifices.

The moment to speak came in the late afternoon, after Vespers. Daddy was sitting on the edge of the cistern. He sat with folded hands gazing on the loveliness of nature: the sun, its midday heat lost, gilded the treetops and the birds joyously sang their evening hymn. Daddy's face had a heavenly look and I felt that his soul was completely at peace. I went and sat beside him without saying a word. There were tears in my eyes. He looked at me tenderly, pressed my head against his breast, and said: "What's the matter, my little queen? Tell me." He got up as if to hide his own emotion and began to walk slowly up and down, holding me close to him. Through my tears I told him of my wanting to enter Carmel. His tears mingled with mine, but he said no word to turn me from my vocation. All he said was that I was still very young to make so serious a decision, but I pleaded my cause so well that his simple, upright nature was soon convinced that my desire came from God. His great faith made him exclaim that God honoured him greatly by asking him to surrender his children. We walked up and down for a long time, and I was happy because of the kindness with which my incomparable father had received my avowal. He seemed to feel that tranquil joy which comes from a sacrifice which has been freely accepted. We went up to a low wall where he showed me some small white flowers looking like miniature lilies. He picked one and gave it me, telling me with what care God had created it and preserved it until that day. As I listened to him I thought I was hearing the story of my own life, so great was the similarity between what Jesus had done for this little flower and for little Thérèse. I took the flower as if it were a relic. I saw that Daddy had picked it without breaking any of its roots, so it seemed as if it were destined to grow on in a more fertile soil than the velvety moss where it had spent its early days. Daddy had just done a similar thing for me in letting me go to the mountain of Carmel and leave the gentle valley of my childhood. I put the little white flower in *The Imitation* at the chapter headed: "Love of Jesus." It is still there, but its stem is broken near the root—by which God seems to tell me that He will soon break the bonds of His little flower and not leave her to wither away down here on earth.

Having got Daddy's consent, I thought I could fly to Carmel without hindrance, but there were many grievous trials ahead to test my vocation. It was in fear and trembling that I told my uncle of what I had decided. He showered me with all possible love and affection, but he did not give me his permission to enter Carmel. In fact, he forbade me to speak to him of my vocation until I was seventeen. He said it was against all human prudence to allow a child of fifteen to enter Carmel. To let an inexperienced child enter would do great harm to religion. He even said that it would need a miracle to make him change his mind. I saw that reasoning with him was useless, so I left him with my heart plunged in the depth of misery. Prayer was my only comfort. I beseeched Jesus to perform this miracle, as it alone would enable me to respond to His call. Some time went by before I ventured to speak to my uncle again and it cost me a good deal to force myself to go to his house. But he seemed as if he wasn't thinking any more about my vocation, though I learned a long time afterwards that my unhappiness greatly influenced him in my favour. But instead of letting me see any ray of hope, God afflicted me with a most grievous martyrdom which lasted for three days. It brought sharply home to me the bitter grief felt by the Blessed Virgin and St. Joseph as they searched for the Child Jesus. I was alone in a desert waste—or rather, my soul was like a fragile skiff tossing without a pilot in a stormy sea. I knew that Jesus was there, asleep in my craft, but the night was too black for me to see Him. All was darkness. Not even a flash of lightning pierced the clouds. There's nothing reassuring about lightning, but, at least, if the storm had burst, I should have been able to glimpse Jesus. But it was night, the dark night of the soul. Like Jesus during His Agony in the Garden, I felt myself abandoned and there was no help for me on earth or in heaven. God had abandoned me. Nature herself seemed to share my misery. The sun never shone once during those three days and the rain fell in torrents. I have noticed that, at all the important moments of my life, nature has mirrored my soul. When I wept the sky wept with me, and when I was happy the sun shone without a cloud in the sky.

I went to see my uncle on the fourth day. It was a Saturday. I was astonished when he took me into his study, for I hadn't asked to see him privately. He began by gently reproaching me for seeming to be afraid of him and then went on to say there was no need to ask for a miracle. He had prayed to God to dispose his heart aright and his prayer was answered. My uncle wasn't the same man. He made no further mention of human prudence, but told me I was a little flower whom God wished to pluck and that he would offer no opposition.

After getting my uncle's consent, I walked joyfully back to Les Buissonnets beneath a lovely sky from which every cloud had vanished. And the night within my soul had also gone. Jesus had awakened, joy had returned, and I no longer heard the noise of the waves. The tempest of my ordeal was replaced by a gentle breeze which filled my sail, and I believed that I should soon reach the blessed haven which now seemed so near. And near it was, but more than one storm was still to rage and there were times when I feared I should be swept for ever from the shore I so longed to reach.

Soon after my uncle had given his consent, you, Pauline, told me the Superior of Carmel would not let me enter before I was twenty-one. No one had foreseen this opposition, and it was the most serious and unyielding of all. I didn't lose heart, though, and went with Father to see him. He was very cold and nothing we said made him change his mind. We finally left him still saying a most decided no. But he did add: "But I'm only the Bishop's deputy. If he allows you to enter, I shall say nothing more." Outside the presbytery, the rain was pouring down and my soul was as overcast with clouds as the sky. Daddy didn't know what to do to comfort me. He offered to take me to Bayeux. I gratefully accepted.

But a lot of things happened before we could go. Outwardly my life seemed the same. I carried on with my studies and I grew in the love of God. Sometimes I experienced true transports of ecstasy.

One evening, not knowing how to tell Jesus how much I loved Him and how much I longed for Him to be served and honoured everywhere, I thought with sadness that not a single act of love ever ascended from the gulfs of hell. I cried that I would gladly be plunged into that realm of blasphemy and pain so that even there He could be loved for ever. Of course that could not glorify Him, for all He wants is our happiness, yet when one's in love one says a thousand silly things. This didn't mean that I did not want to be in heaven, but for me heaven meant love and, in my ardour, I felt that nothing could separate me from Him who had captivated me.

It was about this time that Our Lord gave me some insight into the souls of children. I spent a lot of time looking after two girls during their mother's illness. The elder was not yet six. It was a real delight to see how they believed all I told them. Baptism must sow a vigorous seed of the theological virtues in the soul, for even in childhood the hope of future joy is enough to make present sacrifices acceptable. I didn't promise these two little girls toys and candies to make them stop quarrelling; I told them that good children were given an everlasting reward by the Child Jesus. The elder one was just beginning to think and her face lit up with joy as she asked me scores of fascinating questions about Jesus and His wonderful heaven. She eagerly promised that she would always give way to her sister and said she would never, never forget the teaching of "the tall young lady"—which was what she used to call me.

Those innocent souls were like soft wax on which any imprint could be stamped—of evil, alas, as well as of good. I understood the words of Jesus: "If anyone hurts the conscience of one of these little ones, he had better have been drowned in the depths of the sea." Many, many souls would become most holy if they had been properly guided from the very start.

I know God needs no help to carry out His work of sanctification. He lets a skilled gardener rear rare and delicate plants. He has given him the necessary knowledge, but He fertilises them Himself. That is exactly how He wishes to be helped in cultivating souls.

What would happen if a clumsy gardener did not graft his trees properly? Or if he tried to make roses bloom on a peach tree?

I'm reminded now of a canary I had among my birds. It sang marvellously. I also had a linnet of which I was particularly fond, as I'd had it since it was a fledgling. It had had no singing lessons from its parents and it heard nothing all day but the canary's song. So he tried to imitate him—not very easy for a linnet! It was charming to watch the efforts of the little thing. It obviously found it extremely hard to make its own voice harmonize with the vibrant notes of its master, but to my great surprise its song did in time become exactly like the canary's.

You know, Mother, who has taught me to sing from childhood. You know whose were the voices which charmed me. In spite of all my frailty, I hope that one day I shall begin to sing eternally that canticle of love whose harmonious notes I have so often heard down here below.

But all these thoughts have led me away from my subject. I'll go on at once with the story of my vocation.

Daddy and I set out for Bayeux on October 31, 1887. I was full of hope, but also very nervous at the thought of appearing at the Bishop's palace. For the first time in my life I was going to pay a visit without having any of my sisters with me—and the visit was to a bishop! I'd never had to speak before except to answer questions and now I was going to have to explain and enlarge on my reasons for seeking to enter Carmel. I had to prove my vocation was a real one.

What it cost me to overcome my shyness. It's absolutely true that "nothing is impossible to love, for love is convinced it may and can do all things." And indeed nothing but the love of Jesus enabled me to face these difficulties and those which followed. I suffered much to win my happiness. Now I consider the price very cheap, and to win this happiness—if I hadn't got it—I'd be willing to suffer a thousand times more.

The rain was pouring down when we arrived at the palace. The Vicar-General, Father Révérony, who had arranged the meeting, was very pleasant. When he saw the tears in my eyes, he said: "You mustn't let the Bishop see those diamonds!"

We walked through some huge rooms and I felt about the size of an ant. All the time I was wondering what I dared say. The Bishop was walking along a corridor with two priests; I saw the Vicar-General have a word with him, then come along with him to the room where we were waiting. Three vast armchairs stood before a roaring fire.

As the Bishop entered, Daddy and I knelt for his blessing, and then he asked us to sit down. Father Révérony offered me the armchair in the middle. I politely declined it, but he insisted. He said I must show I knew how to be obedient. So I took it without another word. I was embarrassed to see him take an ordinary chair as I was buried in one so enormous that four girls would have been comfortable in it—much more comfortable than I was! I had hoped Daddy would do the talking, but he asked me to explain the reason for our visit. I spoke as eloquently as I could, all the time knowing very well that a word from the Superior would have helped me more than all my talk. His opposition weighed strongly against me.

The Bishop asked if I had wanted to enter Carmel for a long time.

"Oh yes, Monseigneur, for a very long time."

Father Révérony laughed.

"Come, come," he said. "It can hardly have been for fifteen years."

"That's true," I replied, "but it's not much less, for I've longed to give myself to God ever since I was three."

The Bishop tried to persuade me that I ought to stay at home for some time longer. He obviously thought this would please Daddy and he was both astonished and edified when Daddy took my part and said, with proper deference, that we intended to go to Rome with the diocesan pilgrimage and that I should not hesitate to speak to the Holy Father if I did not get permission beforehand.

Before reaching any decision, the Bishop insisted on discussing the matter with the Superior. Nothing could have upset me more, for I knew just how determined his opposition was. So, forgetting what Father Révérony had said, I began to cry. I saw the Bishop was moved and he showed me greater kindness, I was told later, than he had ever done to any other child.

He told me: "All is not lost, my child. I am delighted you are going to Rome with your father. Your vocation will be strengthened. You should rejoice instead of weeping. Besides, I am going to Lisieux next week and I shall have a talk about you with the Superior. You will have my decision while you're in Italy."

He then took us into the garden and he was most interested when Daddy told him that I had that morning put up my hair for the first time so that I should appear older than I was. This story was not forgotten. Even today the Bishop never speaks to anyone about his "little girl" without telling the story of my hair. I must confess I wish Daddy had said nothing about it. The Vicar-General came with us to the door. He said nothing like it had ever been known: a father as eager to give his child to God as the child was to offer herself.

So we had to return to Lisieux without a favourable reply. I felt my future was finally ruined. The nearer I got to my goal, the more difficulties there were. Yet I felt at peace, for I sought only to do the will of God.

CHAPTER SIX

Three days after my journey to Bayeux I started on a much longer one—to Rome. It was a journey which showed me the emptiness of all temporal things. But I saw splendid monuments and gazed at all the glory of art in the service of religion. Above all, my feet walked on the ground sanctified by the apostles and on the earth drenched by the blood of martyrs. And all these holy things enriched my soul.

Although I was delighted to be going to Rome, I knew that people imagined Father had planned the journey with a view to changing my mind about becoming a nun. And it certainly would have shaken a weak vocation.

The pilgrimage was made up almost entirely of people of birth and position. It was the first time Céline and I had found ourselves among such people. But we weren't dazzled by them, for all their titles seemed quite empty and meaningless. I understood those words of *The Imitation*: "Be not solicitous for the shadow of a great name." I understood that true greatness has nothing to do with a title. It's a matter of the soul.

The prophet Isaias says that God "will have a new name for his own servants," and in St. John we read that to the victor God will give "a white stone, on which stone a new name is written, known to him only who receives it." It is in heaven that we shall know our titles of nobility. Then "each of us will receive his due award from God." The first, the most noble, and the richest will be he who on earth chose to be the poorest and least known for love of Our Lord.

Another discovery I made concerned priests. Until then I hadn't been able to understand the main purpose of Carmel. I loved praying for sinners, but I was astounded at having to pray for priests. I thought their souls were without blemish. It was in Italy that I came to understand my vocation, and it wasn't too far to travel to learn that. I met many holy priests during the month I was away, but I saw that some of them were still men, weak and subject to human frailty, even though the sublime dignity of the priesthood raised them above the angels. Now if prayers are needed for those holy priests whom Jesus called "the salt of the earth," how much more is it needed for priests of lukewarm virtue. For did not Jesus also ask: "If salt loses its taste, what is there left to give taste to?" What a wonderful vocation we Carmelites have! It is up to us to preserve the salt of the earth. We offer our prayers and penance for God's apostles and we are their apostles, while, by word and deed, they bring the Gospel to our brethren. But I must stop writing about this, though I could go on writing about it for ever.

And now, darling Mother, I'm going to describe my journey.

We went to the station at Lisieux at three o'clock in the morning of November 4. I felt I was heading for the unknown, but I knew that what awaited me was of tremendous importance.

In Paris, Daddy took us on a tour of all the famous sights, but for me there was only one: Our Lady of Victories. I can't describe what I experienced in this sanctuary of hers. The graces she gave me were like those of my first Communion. I was filled with joy and peace. And there the Blessed Virgin, my Mother, told me clearly that it really was she who had smiled on me and healed me. I beseeched her to protect me always and to fulfil my longing to hide myself beneath her spotless mantle. I knew that during my absence from home I might come across many things able to unsettle me. I knew nothing of evil, so I was afraid to meet it. I had not yet found out that nothing can be "unclean for those who have clean hearts," and that a simple, virtuous soul sees evil in nothing, for evil exists not in things but in corrupt hearts. I also asked St. Joseph to watch over me for, since early childhood, my love for him had been inseparable from my love for the Blessed Virgin. Every day I uttered the prayer: "O St. Joseph, father and protector of virgins . . ." So I felt well looked after and safe from harm.

After our consecration to the Sacred Heart in the Basilica of Montmartre, we left Paris on November 7. Each compartment of the train was named after a saint, and to honour the priest in that compartment the name of his patron or that of his parish was chosen. In the presence of all the pilgrims, ours was called St. Martin. Daddy was very moved by this compliment and at once went to thank the director of the pilgrimage, Monseigneur Legoux, the Vicar-General of Coutances. Ever afterwards several people always called him "Monsieur St. Martin."

Father Révérony kept a close watch on me—even from a distance. At mealtimes, when I was not sitting opposite him, he kept leaning forward to see me and hear what I was saying. I think he was satisfied with what he saw and heard, for he seemed well disposed to me by the end of the pilgrimage. I say by the end of the pilgrimage, for, as I shall describe soon, he was not at all helpful to me when we were in Rome.

On our way to Rome we crossed Switzerland and saw its mountains with their snow-covered summits lost in clouds, its waterfalls, its deep valleys thick with huge ferns and purple heather. It was wonderfully good for me to see all the richness of this natural loveliness. My soul soared up to Him who delights to scatter such masterpieces over the place where we spend our brief time of exile. Sometimes we were carried up to the mountain peaks, and precipices, whose depths our eyes could not plumb, opened at our feet as if to engulf us. Then we passed through a charming village, with its chalets and graceful church spire over which wisps of cloud were drifting. Later the blue waters of a great lake, calm and clear, would catch the glory of the setting sun.

But how can I describe what I felt before the wonder and the poetry of these scenes? They were a foretaste of the splendours of heaven. I saw life in a convent as it really is, with all its restrictions and its little daily hidden sacrifices. I realised how easy it would be to become wrapped up in oneself and to forget the sublime purpose of our vocation. I said: "Later, in the hour of trial and when I am imprisoned in Carmel and able to see only a small patch of sky, I shall recall today and it will give me strength. All my trifling affairs will be lost in the power and majesty of God. I shall love only Him and I shall escape the misfortune of attaching myself to trifles, now that I have glimpsed what He has in store for those who love Him."

Besides the works of God, I was able to admire those of His creatures. Milan was the first Italian city we came to. We visited, of course, its cathedral of white marble which has enough statues to populate a town. Some of the ladies of our party were afraid to climb more than the first flight of the stairs inside the cathedral, but Céline and I followed the braver pilgrims and reached the roof. From there we saw the whole city at our feet and people moving about like ants. When we were down on the ground again, we began those carriage drives which went on for a month. They've completely cured me from wanting to ride around at my ease.

The cemetery fascinated us. Its whole vast area is covered with statues dotted about in an attractively casual manner. Only the chisel of genius could have made them so lifelike. I felt I almost had to comfort all these figures which surrounded us, their expression of calm, Christian grief was so realistic. They were masterpieces. We saw a child scattering flowers on his father's grave and we quite forgot that the petals which seemed to slip through his fingers were of marble. And the windows' veils and the ribbons in the hair of the statues of girls seemed to stir in the breeze. We couldn't express our admiration in words. An old gentleman—he was a Frenchman—used to follow us around everywhere, and in this cemetery he exclaimed rather testily: "How enthusiastic the French are!" No doubt he regretted not being able to share our feelings, but I think he would have been better off at home. For, far from getting any pleasure out of the journey, he never stopped complaining. He disliked the towns, the hotels, the people—everything.

Daddy was just the opposite, for he was always happy no matter where he was, and he tried to cheer up this disagreeable character. He offered him his seat in the carriage and, with his usual good nature, tried to make him look on the bright side of things. But nothing would cheer him up. What a varied collection of people we met and how fascinating the world is when one is on the point of leaving it!

Venice was very different from Milan. The noise of a great city gave place to a silence broken only by the shouts of the gondoliers and the splash of their oars. It's a charming but melancholy place. Even the Palace of the Doges, with all its splendour, is full of gloom. We walked through halls whose vaulted roofs long ago ceased to echo the ruler's voice giving a man his life or sending him to death. The wretched victims no longer suffer a living death in the underground dungeons. When I saw those frightful cells, I thought I was back in the days of the martyrs and I would joyfully have endured their horrors to witness to my faith. The voice of my guide soon broke in on my daydream, and I went on to walk over the Bridge of Sighs, so called from the sighs of relief that came from the prisoners going to the death they preferred to the horrors of imprisonment.

After leaving Venice, we arrived in Padua where we venerated St. Anthony's tongue and, at Bologna, the body of St. Catherine whose face is marked with the kiss of the Child Jesus.

I was full of happiness when we set off to Loreto. The Blessed Virgin chose well when she placed her house there. Everything is primitive, poor, and simple. The women still wear the charming native dress, unlike those of other towns who follow the fashions of Paris. Loreto enchanted me. What shall I say about the holy house? I was deeply moved to be under the very roof which had sheltered the Holy Family, and to be looking at the walls on which Our Lord had gazed and walking on the ground once moistened by St. Joseph's sweat, and to be where Mary had carried Jesus in her arms after carrying Him in her virginal womb. I saw the little room of the Annunciation and I put my rosary in the dish used by the Child Jesus. I have very dear memories of it all.

Our greatest happiness came when we received Jesus in His own house and became His living temple in the very spot glorified by His divine Presence. It's the Roman custom that the Blessed Eucharist is received at only one altar in each church and the priests give It to the faithful only at that particular altar. At Loreto the altar is in the Basilica which encloses the holy house like a casket of white marble round a precious diamond. This arrangement didn't suit us at all. We wanted to receive the Bread of Angels in the diamond itself, not in its casket. Daddy, docile as usual, went with the rest of the pilgrims, but his less docile daughters went into the holy house. A priest who had a special privilege was getting ready to say Mass there, so we told him what we wanted and he at once asked for two Hosts and placed them on the paten. You can imagine the indescribable, wonderful joy of that Communion. What will it be like when we enjoy a never-ending Communion in the mansion of the King of Heaven? Then our delight will be without end and without a shadow; we shall not have to scratch fragments furtively from the walls made holy by the divine Presence—as we did at Loreto—for His dwelling place will be our home throughout the ages. He lets us see His earthly home so that we may love poverty and the hidden life, but He conceals the palace where He dwells in glory. There we shall no longer see Him veiled beneath the appearance of a baby or a piece of bread, but in the full light of His infinite splendour.

Now I'm going to write about Rome—Rome where I thought I should get comfort, but where I found a cross instead. We arrived at night. I was asleep and was roused by the shouts of the porters, joyfully taken up by the pilgrims: "Rome! Rome!" I wasn't dreaming. I was in Rome.

We spent our first day—perhaps the nicest—outside the walls. All the monuments there still have their air of antiquity, but the hotels and shops in the centre of the city make one think of Paris. The trip through the Campagna left me with one very precious memory. I can't possibly describe the emotion which set me trembling as I stood before the Coliseum and I saw at last the arena where so many martyrs had shed their blood for Jesus. I longed to kiss the ground sanctified by their glorious combats. But how disappointed I was! The level of the soil had been raised so that the actual arena now lies some eight yards below the surface. Excavations have covered the centre with piles of rubble and a barrier prevented our getting to it. No one dared to venture into the heart of those dangerous ruins. But to have come all the way to Rome without going down into the arena was impossible. I stopped listening to our guide. I thought of one thing only—how to get into the arena.

The Gospel says Mary Magdalene stayed close to the Sepulchre and, stooping constantly to look inside, at last saw two angels. Like her, I continued to stoop and saw, not two angels but what I was looking for. With a cry of joy I shouted to Céline: "Come on! Follow me! We can get down!" We rushed off together, clambering over the ancient stonework which crumbled under our feet, whilst Daddy, startled by our rashness, shouted after us. But we heard nothing. Like those warriors whose courage grows with danger, our joy increased in face of the tiredness and perils we had to face to reach the goal of our desire.

Céline had shown more sense than I in listening to the guide. She remembered he had mentioned a small paving stone marked with a cross which was the place where the martyrs died. She started looking for it and soon found it. We knelt on the sacred spot and our souls joined in the same prayer. My heart beat fast as I pressed my lips to the dust reddened by the blood of the first Christians. I begged that I too might be a martyr for Jesus, and I felt deep within me that my prayer was granted. All this didn't last very long. We picked up a few stones and began our perilous journey back. We looked so happy that Daddy couldn't scold us; in fact, I saw that he was very proud of our courage.

We next visited the Catacombs. Céline and I managed to lie

down together in the ancient tomb of St. Cecilia and we carried off some of the earth sanctified by her holy relics. Up to then I had no special devotion for this saint. But after visiting her house where she was martyred, and after hearing her proclaimed "queen of harmony" because of that pure song which rose to her divine Spouse from the depth of her heart, I felt more than a devotion for her: I felt the real tenderness of a friend. She became my favourite saint and I confided everything to her. What especially delighted me was her abandonment to God and her boundless confidence in Him. They enabled her to make souls virginally pure which had previously desired only the joys of this present life. St. Cecilia is like the spouse in the Canticles. Her life was nothing but a lovely song in the midst of terrible trials. It does not surprise me, for the "Holy Gospel reposed on her heart," and in her heart the Spouse of Virgins rested.

Our visit to the church of St. Agnes also made me very happy. There I met again a friend of my childhood. I tried in vain to get a relic for you, my dear Mother Agnes of Jesus. They refused me one, but then God took a hand in it: a small fragment of red marble fell at my feet. It came from a gorgeous mosaic dating back to the time of the martyrs. Wasn't it wonderful for St. Agnes herself to give me a souvenir of her house?

We spent six more days looking at the wonders of Rome, and on the seventh I saw the greatest of them all: Leo XIII. I both longed for and dreaded that day, for the fulfilment of my vocation depended on it. I had had no word from the Bishop of Bayeux, and my only hope lay in getting the Holy Father's permission. But to get it I had to ask for it. I should have to speak to the Pope in front of cardinals, archbishops, and bishops. I trembled at the thought.

On Sunday morning, November 20, we went to the Vatican, and at eight o'clock we heard Mass in the Chapel of the Sovereign

Pontiff. During the Mass his ardent piety, worthy of the Vicar of Jesus Christ, showed us how truly he was our Holy Father.

The Gospel for the day had these moving words: "Do not be afraid, you, my little flock. Your Father has determined to give you His kingdom." I felt full of confidence. I lost my fear and hoped that the kingdom of Carmel would soon be mine. I didn't think of those other words of Jesus: "As my Father has allotted a kingdom to me, so I allot to you a place to eat and drink at my table in my kingdom." In other words, there are crosses and trials for you and they will make you worthy of my kingdom. "Was it not to be expected that the Christ should undergo these sufferings, and enter so into His glory? If you desire to sit on His right hand, you must drink the chalice which He has drunk Himself."

The audience began after the Mass of thanksgiving which followed the Pope's Mass.

Leo XIII sat on a dais, dressed in a white cape and cassock. Various prelates and high dignitaries stood near him. It had been arranged that, one by one, each pilgrim advance and kneel before him, kiss first his foot and then his hand, and receive his blessings. Then, at a touch from two of the Noble Guard, the pilgrim was to rise and move on to another room, thus giving way to another.

Not a word was uttered, but I was determined to speak. Suddenly, though, Father Révérony, who was standing on the right of His Holiness, told us in a loud voice that it was absolutely forbidden to speak to the Holy Father. With a madly beating heart I gave a questioning glance at Céline. "Speak!" she whispered. A moment later I was kneeling before the Pope. I kissed his slipper and he offered me his hand. Then, looking at him with my eyes wet with tears, I said: "Most Holy Father, I have a great favour to ask." He leant forward until his face almost touched mine, as if his dark, searching eyes would pierce the depths of my soul.

"Most Holy Father," I said, "to mark your jubilee, allow me to enter Carmel at fifteen."

The Vicar-General of Bayeux, with a look of astonished displeasure, at once said: "Most Holy Father, she's a child who wants to be a Carmelite, and the authorities are now looking into the matter."

"Very well, my child," His Holiness said, "do whatever they say."

Clasping my hands and resting them on his knee, I made a final effort. "O most Holy Father, if you say yes, everybody will be only too willing."

He gazed at me steadily and said in a clear voice, stressing every syllable: "Come, come . . . you will enter if God wills."

I was going to speak again, but the two Noble Guards urged me to rise. Finally they had to take me by the arms and Father Révérony helped them to get me to my feet. As I was being taken away, the Holy Father placed his fingers on my lips, then raised them to bless me. He gazed after me as I left.

Daddy was very upset when he saw my tears as I came from the audience. As his turn was before mine, he knew nothing about my pleas to the Pope. As far as Father was concerned, the Vicar-General could not have been more pleasant and he presented him to Leo XIII as the father of two Carmelite nuns. The Sovereign Pontiff, as a mark of special benevolence, laid his hand on his venerable head as if to place on it a mystic seal in the name of Christ Himself. Now this father of *four* Carmelite nuns is in heaven, the hand of the representative of Jesus on his brow has been replaced by that of the Spouse of Virgins, the King of Heaven, and never will that divine Hand be withdrawn from the head It has glorified.

My suffering was severe, but as I had done absolutely everything that I myself could do to answer God's call, I must admit that, in spite of all my tears, I felt a great peace deep down within me. Yet this inner peace did not prevent my feeling an immense sorrow. And Jesus was silent. He seemed to have left me and nothing revealed His presence to me.

That day the sun dared not shine, and from the gloomy clouds which covered the blue Italian sky the rain poured down as I wept. Everything was over: all the pleasure had gone from my journey, as the whole point of it had just been destroyed. Yet the final words of the Holy Father should have comforted me, for they were truly prophetic. In spite of every obstacle, God's will was accomplished. His will triumphed over that of human beings.

For some time I had been accustomed to offer myself as a plaything to the Child Jesus. I told Him not to treat me like an expensive toy which children look at but dare not touch. I was a cheap little ball which He could fling on the ground or kick or pierce or leave neglected in a corner or even press to His Heart if it gave Him pleasure. To put it in a nutshell, I longed to amuse the little Jesus and offer myself to His childish whims.

He answered my prayer. In Rome, Jesus pierced His little toy. He wanted to see what was inside and then, having found out, He let His little ball drop and went to sleep. What did He dream about and what happened to the abandoned ball? Jesus dreamt that He was still playing with it, picking it up and dropping it, letting it roll away from Him, but in the end pressing it close to His Heart and never letting it slip again from His little Hand. You can understand, Mother, how sad the little ball was to see itself lying on the ground, but she went on hoping against all hope.

A few days after my plea to the Pope Father paid a visit to Brother Simeon, the founder and director of St. Joseph's College. There he met Father Révérony. He gently reproached him for not having helped me in my difficult undertaking and then told my story to Brother Simeon. The good old man listened with great interest, made some notes about it, and said with feeling: "One doesn't see that kind of thing in Italy!"

The day after the audience we left for Naples and Pompeii. Vesuvius honoured us with several salvoes and sent up a dense column of smoke from its crater. What the volcano did to Pompeii is terrifying. It shows the power of God whose "glance makes earth tremble; at his touch, the mountains are wreathed in smoke." I should have loved to wander alone among the ruins, meditating on the frailty of human things, but it was quite impossible.

From Naples we made a wonderful excursion to the Monastery of San Martino which stands on a hill overlooking the whole city. On our way back the horses bolted, but our guardian angels brought us back safe and sound to our magnificent hotel. I used the word "magnificent" deliberately, for every hotel we stayed in was fit for a king. I'd never before known such luxury. Yet how true it is that wealth doesn't bring happiness. I should have been a thousand times happier under a thatched roof with the prospect of Carmel before me than living in a palace with a marble staircase and silken hangings and yet having this sorrow in my heart. I realised very clearly that happiness has nothing to do with the material things which surround us; it dwells in the very depths of the soul. One can be just as happy in a gloomy prison as in a palace. I am much happier in Carmel, even though I suffer spiritual trials and the ordinary inconveniences of life here, than I ever was outside where I wanted for nothing and enjoyed all the comforts of home.

Although my distress was so great, I let nothing of it show, for I thought I had kept my plea to the Holy Father a secret. I soon found I was wrong. I was in the railway carriage alone with Céline one day, while the other pilgrims had gone to the buffet, when Monseigneur Legoux appeared at the door. He took a good look at me and then, with a smile, asked: "How is our little Carmelite?" I knew then that the whole pilgrimage knew my secret, and I saw people giving me sympathetic glances. Fortunately no one spoke to me about it.

I had a little adventure in Assisi. After we had visited the spots blessed by the holiness of St. Francis and St. Clare, I found I had lost the buckle of my belt in the monastery. By the time I had found it and put it on, all the carriages but one had gone—and that one was the carriage of the Vicar-General of Bayeux! What was I to do? Run after the other carriages which, by then, were out of sight and so risk missing the train, or ask for a seat in Father Révérony's carriage? I decided to do the sensible thing. Although most embarrassed, I tried not to show it as I explained what had happened. And then he was embarrassed, for there wasn't a spare seat in the carriage. But one of the gentlemen at once got out and made me take his place while he sat with the coachman. I was like a fish out of water and felt extremely uneasy surrounded by all those important people and sitting exactly opposite the most formidable of them. But he was charming, breaking off his talk with the others to speak to me of Carmel. He assured me he would do all he could to help me to fulfil my ambition to enter it at fifteen.

This meeting comforted me, but it did not end all my suffering, for I had no faith in human aid and could depend no longer on anyone but God. Yet my unhappiness didn't stop my taking a keen interest in the holy places we visited. I enjoyed looking at St. Magdalene of Pazzi in the middle of the choir of the Carmelites at Florence. All the pilgrims wanted to touch her tomb with their rosaries, but only my hand was small enough to pass through the grille. So I undertook this honourable task. It took quite a time and made me very proud.

It was not the first time I'd enjoyed such a privilege. At Rome, in the church of the Holy Cross of Jerusalem, we venerated some fragments of the true Cross, two thorns, and one of the sacred nails. I stayed behind so that I could take my time in looking at them. When the monk in charge of these treasures came to restore them to the altar, I asked if I could touch them. He said I could, but seemed to think I shouldn't be able to. I pushed my little finger into a hole in the reliquary and was just able to touch the precious nail stained with the Blood of Jesus. As you can see, I behaved towards Jesus like a child who thinks she's allowed to do anything and regards her father's treasures as her own.

After passing through Pisa and Genoa, we returned to France by a most beautiful route. Sometimes we ran alongside the sea, and once, during a storm, it seemed as if the waves were going to wash over us. Later we passed great orchards of oranges and olives and groves of gracious palm trees. At evening the glittering lights of the ports came on as the first stars shone in the darkening sky. I saw these fairylike scenes vanish without regret, for my heart was set on another kind of loveliness.

Daddy suggested I should go on another pilgrimage, this time to Jerusalem. I felt a natural longing to visit the places sanctified by the steps of Our Lord, but I was weary of earthly pilgrimages. I wanted nothing but the splendours of heaven and, in order that I could give them to other souls, I wanted to become a prisoner in Carmel as soon as possible. I felt certain that I should still have to struggle and suffer before the doors of this blessed prison would open to receive me. Yet I remained confident and I expected to enter Carmel on Christmas Day.

We had hardly got back to Lisieux before we went to Carmel. And what a meeting it was! I'm sure you remember it. I put myself completely in your hands, for I had exhausted all my resources. You told me to write to the Bishop and remind him of his promise. I obeyed at once. The moment the letter was in the post, I thought there wouldn't be a moment's delay before I got permission to enter Carmel. But as the days went by I saw how mistaken I was. The lovely feast of Christmas came and Jesus still slept. He left His little ball lying on the ground and never even gave it a glance.

It was a very great trial, but He whose Heart never sleeps taught me that He performs miracles for someone whose faith is like a tiny mustard seed. He does this to strengthen a faith so weak, but for His close friends and for His Mother He works no miracles before testing their faith. He let Lazarus die, though Martha and Mary had sent word that he was ill. And at the wedding feast at Cana the Blessed Virgin asked Jesus to help the master of the house, but she was told that His hour had not yet come. But what a reward they got when the water was turned into wine and Lazarus rose from the dead! Jesus dealt thus with His little Thérèse. He fulfilled all her desires, but only after a long period of testing her faith.

For my New Year's gift on January 1, 1888, Jesus gave me a cross. Mother Marie of Gonzaga wrote and said she had had the Bishop's reply since December 28, the Feast of the Holy Innocents, and that it authorised my immediate entry. She, however, had decided to make me wait until after Easter. I wept at the thought of so long a delay. This trial was most severe: my links with the world were snapped and now the Holy Ark refused to take in the poor little dove.

How did I spend those three months? They were rich in suffering and most valuable for spiritual favours of every kind. At first I thought I ought to relax and lead a less constricted life than usual, but God made me realise what benefit I could get from this time of waiting. I resolved to lead a life of greater devoutness and mortification than ever before. When I speak of mortification, I don't mean the kind of penance practised by saints. There are great souls who practise every sort of mortification from childhood, but I am not like them. All I did was to break my self-will, check a hasty reply, and do little kindnesses without making a fuss about them— and lots of other similar things. So I prepared myself to become the bride of Jesus and no words can tell how this wait increased my humility and self-abnegation.

CHAPTER SEVEN

The day chosen for my entry was Monday, April 9, 1888. Carmel was celebrating the Feast of the Annunciation which had been put back because of Easter. The evening before we all gathered round the family table where I sat for the last time. Moments of farewell are heartbreaking and I longed to be ignored. Everyone, though, spoke to me so tenderly that the pain of separation was made even sharper.

I left for Carmel next morning, after a last glance at Les Buissonnets where I had spent so many happy hours. I heard Mass in the midst of my dear relatives. They were all sobbing as they received Jesus in Holy Communion. I shed no tears, but as I walked to the door of the enclosure my heart beat so violently that I thought I should die.

The agony of such a moment has to be experienced to be understood.

I kissed all my relatives and knelt before Father to receive his blessing. He knelt himself and blessed me as he wept. To see this old man offering God his child, still in the springtime of her life, was a sight to make the angels rejoice. Then at last the doors of Carmel closed behind me and I was embraced by those beloved sisters who had been like mothers to me and by a whole new family whose love and tenderness is little guessed at by the world outside.

So my longing was at last fulfilled. I knew a deep and serene peace beyond description. For eight and a half years this peace has been mine and it has never left me even in the midst of the most severe trials.

Everything in the convent charmed me. My little cell gave me special pleasure. Yet, I repeat, it was a tranquil happiness I knew and not the slightest breeze ruffled the peaceful waters over which my little boat moved. Not a single cloud darkened my sky. I was fully recompensed for all I had suffered and it was with profound joy that I said to myself over and over again: "Now I am here for good!"

There was nothing transitory about my happiness and it wasn't an illusion which disappeared after my first few weeks in the convent. For God, in his mercy, has preserved me from illusions. I found that a nun's life was just what I imagined it would be. None of its sacrifices surprised me, and yet, as you know, Mother, there were at first more thorns than roses on my path.

For one thing, I suffered from grievous spiritual dryness. And, in addition, Our Lord allowed the prioress to treat me with great severity, though she didn't always realise it. I never met her without being reprimanded for something. I remember once, when I had overlooked a cobweb in the cloister, she said to me in front of all the other nuns: "It's easy to see our cloister is swept by a child of fifteen! Go and sweep the cobweb away and be more careful in future." I was scolded nearly all the time during the hour I spent with her whenever—which was not often—she gave me spiritual direction. What upset me most was that I could not see how to correct my faults—faults such as my slowness and lack of thoroughness.

One day I decided that the prioress wanted me to work during our free hours which were normally devoted to prayer. So I sewed away without taking my eyes from my work, but no one ever knew anything about it, as I wanted to work only under the gaze of Jesus.

Whilst I was a postulant, our novice mistress sent me to weed the garden every afternoon at half past four, and on the way I was almost certain to run into Mother Marie of Gonzaga. On one of these encounters she exclaimed: "But this child does absolutely nothing! What kind of a novice is one that has to be sent for a stroll every day?" And she behaved like that to me about everything.

How I thank God for such firm and valuable training. It was a priceless favour, for what should I have become if I had been the pet of the community—as some people outside the convent thought I was? Instead of seeing Our Lord in my superiors, I should have looked on them as human beings and my heart, so carefully guarded when I was in the world, might have become too involved with human affairs in the cloister. Fortunately I was saved from such a very real misfortune.

I can truthfully say that, as soon as I entered Carmel, suffering stretched out her arms to me and I embraced her lovingly. I say this not only because of what I've just written, but because of other even more painful trials. At the solemn examination before my Profession, I stated what I was going to do in Carmel: "I have come to save souls and, above all, to pray for priests." If one wants to

achieve one's object, one has to use the right means, and as Jesus
had told me He would give me souls through the Cross, I wel-
comed the Cross and my love of suffering grew steadily. For five
years I trod this path, but no one else knew of it. This was the hidden flower I wanted to offer to Jesus, the flower which breathes out
its perfume only in the garden of heaven.

Father Pichon, only two months after my entrance, was astonished at God's dealings with my soul. He trusted my childlike fervour and thought my spiritual way a good and gentle one. I was
greatly comforted by my talk with this good priest, although I
found it extremely hard to express all I felt. But I made a general
confession and afterwards he said: "Before God, the Blessed Virgin,
the angels, and all the saints, I declare that you have never committed a single mortal sin; thank Our Lord for what He has freely done
for you without any merit on your part."

I found it easy to believe I merited nothing, for I knew how
weak I was and how far I was from perfection. Nothing but gratitude filled my heart. I had been suffering a lot from the fear of having stained the white gown of my baptism, and Father Pichon's
assurance seemed to come from God Himself. For he was a spiritual
director such as our foundress, St. Teresa, would have approved—
he was both learned and holy. He also said to me: "My child, may
Our Lord always be your Superior and your Novice Master." And
indeed He was and also my spiritual Director. By this, I don't mean
that I kept my spiritual life a secret from my superiors. Far from
hiding my development, I always tried to be an open book.

The novice mistress was a true saint, a perfect model of the first
Carmelites. I spent most of my time with her, as it was her job to
teach me to work. Her kindness was beyond words. I appreciated all
she did for me and I loved her dearly. Yet I could not be frank with

her. I didn't know how to express what was happening within me, for I was ignorant of the right words for it. So my periods of direction were a torture, a real martyrdom.

One of the old nuns seemed to understand what I was going through. At recreation one day she said: "It strikes me, my child, that you cannot have much to say to your superiors."

"Why do you think that, Mother?"

"Because your soul is very simple, but when you are perfect, you will be more simple still. The nearer one gets to God, the simpler one becomes."

She was right. Nevertheless this tremendous difficulty I had in unburdening myself was a great trial, even though it was because of my simplicity. Although nowadays I am still simple, I express myself with the greatest ease.

I've said that Jesus was my Director. Father Pichon's superiors sent him to Canada almost as soon as he had begun to guide me. I had only one letter a year from him, so I, the Little Flower on the mountain of Carmel, turned at once to the Director of directors and blossomed in the shadow of the Cross. I was watered by His tears and Precious Blood and His adorable Face was my radiant sun.

Until then I had known nothing of the richness of the treasures of the Holy Face and it was you who made me acquainted with them. Just as you were the first of us to enter Carmel, so you were first to explore the mysteries of love hidden in the Face of Jesus. You revealed them to me and I understood more clearly than ever what true glory is. He whose kingdom is not of this world showed me that the only condition worth coveting is "to want to be ignored and regarded as nothing, to find joy in contempt of self." I wanted my face, like the Face of Jesus, to be, as it were, hidden and unrecognised. I longed to suffer and be forgotten.

How thick with mercies is the path along which God has always led me! He has fulfilled every one of my desires, and that is why His bitter cup is sweet to me.

At the end of May, 1888, affliction struck the family again. It was after the Profession of Marie, the eldest of us, whom I, the youngest, had the honour of crowning with roses on that day of her mystical marriage. We had noticed that Father tired very easily ever since his first attack of paralysis. During our visit to Rome I often saw the traces of pain and exhaustion on his face. But what struck me most was his great progress along the path of holiness. He seemed quite untroubled by any worldly affairs. Here's an example of his goodness. During the pilgrimage to Rome some of the pilgrims found the days and nights in the train long and boring. So they used to have card parties which sometimes grew rather rowdy. One day they asked us to join in. We refused, saying we didn't know how to play well enough. For we certainly didn't find the time drag: it was all too short for us to enjoy the magnificent scenery through which we passed. But the card players were annoyed at our refusal, so Father quietly defended our attitude and made it plain that too little time on this pilgrimage was being spent in prayer.

One of the players, forgetting the respect due to Father's age, said without thinking: "It's a good job there are not many Pharisees." Daddy made no reply, and soon afterwards he shook hands with the man and spoke so pleasantly to him that he must have thought his words hadn't been heard or, at least, had been forgotten.

But, as you know, this readiness of Father to forgive did not start then. On the evidence of Mummy and of everybody who knew him, he never once uttered an uncharitable word. Nor did any trial ever shake his faith. This is how he gave a friend news of my departure to Carmel: "Thérèse, my little queen, entered Carmel yesterday. Only God could demand such a sacrifice, but He has helped me to endure it so that, even though I weep, my heart is dancing with joy."

Such a faithful servant of the Lord had to have a reward equal to his virtue. He himself asked God for this reward. You remember when, in this very parlour, he said to us: "I've come from Alençon and the church of Notre Dame. There I received such comfort and such graces that I prayed: 'O Lord, it is too much. I'm too happy. I can't go to heaven in this state. I want to suffer for You.' And I offered myself as . . ." The word "victim" died on his lips, for he dared not utter it in front of us, yet we understood. You remember, Mother, all we suffered and you know what heartbreaking memories we have. There's no need to go into details about it all.

The time came for me to take the habit. Against all expectation, Father had recovered from a second attack of paralysis, and the Bishop chose January 10 for the ceremony. It had been a long wait, but the lovely day came at last. Nothing was missing, not even snow. Have I told you, Mother, of how much I love snow? Its whiteness fascinated me even when I was a tiny child. I wonder how I got this liking for snow. Perhaps because I was a little winter flower and the first thing I saw was the earth adorned with a mantle of white. So, on the day I received the habit, I longed to see the world dressed in white like me. But on the day before it was as mild as spring and I gave up all hope of snow. There was no change by ten o'clock next morning. So I thought there was no chance of my childish longings being fulfilled, and I went out to where Daddy was waiting for me at the door to the enclosure. With tears in his eyes he came to me and hugged me to him. "Ah," he cried, "here is my little queen!" He gave me his arm and we made a solemn entrance into the chapel. It was a day of triumph for him, the last feast he was to enjoy down here. There was nothing left for him to offer. All his family belonged to God, for Céline had told him that she too, in time, would leave the world for Carmel. When he heard that, Father joyfully exclaimed: "Come, we must go together, kneel before the Blessed Sacrament, and give thanks to God for the favour He shows our family and for the honour He does me by choosing His brides from my home. Yes, indeed, God does me great honour by demanding my children from me. And if I had anything of greater worth I should hasten to offer it Him." That something of greater worth was himself. He became God's "gold, tried in the crucible, his burnt sacrifice, graciously accepted."

After the ceremony in the chapel I returned to the enclosure and the Bishop sang the *Te Deum*. A priest said to him that this was sung only at the Ceremony of Profession but, as the hymn had started, it was sung right through to the end. It was fitting, I think, that this should complete the feast, as it was one which embraced all the others.

As I stepped back into the enclosure the first thing I saw was the statue of the Child Jesus smiling at me from the midst of flowers and light of candles. Then, turning towards the quadrangle, *I saw it was completely covered with snow!* How considerate of Jesus! He sent the snow to satisfy the longing of His little bride. Could any man, however powerful, make a single snowflake fall to please his beloved? Everyone was astonished at the snow and thought it most remarkable because of the warm weather. Since then, many who knew how I'd longed for it, have spoken of the "little miracle" of my Clothing Day, though they thought my love of snow was peculiar. So much the better if it was a little peculiar, for it reveals more clearly the inconceivable graciousness of the Spouse of Virgins who loves His lilies to be as white as snow.

After the ceremony the Bishop entered the enclosure and

treated me with fatherly kindness. In front of all the other priests he spoke of my visit to him at Bayeux and of my journey to Rome— without, of course, forgetting to mention how I'd put up my hair. He put his hands on my head and stroked it for a long time as he talked. Our Lord put into my mind—and how sweet the idea was— the thought of how He would lavish caresses on me in the presence of the saints. It was like a foretaste of the glories of heaven.

I've just said that this January tenth was Father's day of triumph. I compare it to the entrance of Jesus into Jerusalem on Palm Sunday. Like his divine Master, his day of glory was followed by a grievous passion and, just as the sufferings of Jesus pierced the Heart of His Mother, so our hearts were torn by the suffering and humiliation of the one we loved more than anyone on earth.

In June, 1888—just when we feared he would suffer a cerebral paralysis—I astonished our novice mistress by saying: "I am suffering a lot, but I feel I can endure much more." I didn't know then of the trial before us. I didn't know that on February 12, a month after my Clothing Day, our dear father would have to drink so bitter a cup. Then I didn't say I could suffer more! Words can't describe our agony, so I shan't try to write about it.

Later, in heaven, we shall enjoy talking of these gloomy days of our exile. For the three years of Father's martyrdom seem to me to have been the sweetest and most fruitful period of our lives. I would not exchange them for the most wonderful ecstasies. In gratitude for the priceless treasure of this suffering my heart cries out: "We have rejoiced for the days in which thou hast humbled us: for the years in which we have seen evils."

O dearest Mother, how sweet and precious this bitter cross was, since we felt nothing but love and gratitude for it. We no longer walked along the way of perfection—we ran, we flew.

Léonie and Céline were no longer of the world, though they

lived in it. The letters they wrote us at this time are filled with an admirable resignation. And what marvellous meetings I had then with Céline in the parlour! The grille, far from separating us, united us still more closely. We were stirred by the same thoughts, the same desires, and the same love for Jesus and for souls. There was never a mention of any earthly affairs in all our talk. We couldn't, as we used to at Les Buissonnets, sit and gaze at the stars, but our souls soared beyond space and, so that we should soon enjoy eternal happiness, we chose to suffer and to be despised on earth.

My longing to suffer was granted to the full, yet its attraction for me never lessened and soon my soul shared the trials of my heart. My spiritual dryness increased and I found no comfort in heaven or earth. And yet, in the midst of this flood of grief I had so eagerly called down on myself, I was as happy as could be. And so the time of my betrothal passed. It was much too long for me. At the end of the year of my novitiate Mother Marie of Gonzaga told me not to think of my Profession, as the Superior had expressly forbidden it. I should have to wait another eight months. At first it was hard to make such a sacrifice, but it wasn't long before divine light illumined my soul.

At this time I was meditating on Father Surin's *Foundations of the Spiritual Life*. One day, as I was praying, I realised that my eager desire to make my vows was mixed with a lot of self-love. As I was the little plaything of Jesus, there to console and amuse Him, I had no business pressing Him to do my will instead of His. I realised too that on her wedding day a bride would not be pleasing to her husband unless she was richly and beautifully dressed, and I knew that I had not yet worked to be attired like such a bride. So I told Our Lord: "I'll not ask You again to hasten my Profession. I'll wait as long as You wish. But I cannot endure that my union with You should be delayed through any fault of mine, and so I am going to put all my energy into making myself a gown adorned with diamonds and every kind of gem. When You think it is rich enough, I am certain that nothing will stop You from taking me as Your bride."

I set myself to the task with new courage. Since my Clothing, much had been revealed to me of religious perfection—mainly about the vow of poverty. Whilst I was a postulant, I got pleasure out of having nice things to use and having everything I needed ready at hand. Jesus bore with this patiently. He does not like to reveal everything at once. He usually enlightens one gradually.

At the start of my spiritual life, when I was thirteen or fourteen, I used to wonder what more I could ever learn about spiritual perfection. I thought it impossible to understand it better. But I soon came to know that the farther one travels along that road, the farther away the goal seems to get. Nowadays I'm resigned to seeing myself in a permanent state of imperfection and I even delight in it.

I'll return to the lessons Our Lord gave me. One evening, after Compline, I looked in vain for my lamp on the shelves where they are kept. As it was the Lent Silence, I couldn't ask for it. I thought—rightly—that a sister had taken it in mistake for hers. So, because of this mistake, I had to spend a whole hour in darkness and it was an evening when I'd planned to do a lot of work. But for the interior light of grace I should certainly have been very sorry for myself. As it was, instead of feeling upset, I rejoiced and thought that true poverty meant being without essentials, not only of pleasant things. And in the darkness of my cell my soul was flooded with divine light.

During this period I was seized with a passion for the ugliest and most inconvenient things. For instance, I was delighted when a pretty little jug in my cell was replaced by a big chipped one. I also tried hard not to make excuses. This was very difficult, especially where our novice mistress was concerned, for I wanted to hide nothing from her.

My first victory was not a big one, but it cost me a great deal. A small vase, which someone had left lying behind a window, was found broken. Our novice mistress thought I was guilty of leaving it lying about. She was cross, told me I was thoroughly untidy, and ordered me to be more careful in future. Without a word, I kissed the ground and promised not to be untidy again. As I've said, these trifles cost me a lot because I was so lacking in virtue, and I had to remember that all would be revealed on the Day of Judgement.

Above all, I tried to do my small good deeds in secret. I loved folding up the mantles forgotten by the sisters and seized every possible opportunity of helping them. I was also attracted towards penance, but I was not allowed to satisfy my longing. The only mortification granted me was to master my self-love, and that did me far more good than any bodily penance.

Meanwhile the Blessed Virgin helped me to adorn the gown for my soul. The moment it was finished, all obstacles vanished and my Profession was fixed for September 8, 1890. All that I have written in a few words really needed pages, but they are pages that will never be read on earth.

CHAPTER EIGHT

Now I'll tell you of the retreat before my Profession. I was far from getting any consolation from it. Instead, I suffered complete spiritual dryness, almost as if I were quite forsaken. As usual, Jesus slept in my little boat. I know that other souls rarely let Him sleep peacefully, and He is so wearied by the advances He is always making that He hastens to take advantage of the rest I offer Him. It's likely that as far as I'm concerned, He will stay asleep until the great final retreat of eternity. But that doesn't upset me. It fills me with great joy. It's true that I'm a long way from being a saint, and this attitude of mine proves it. Instead of delighting in my spiritual aridity, I ought to blame my lack of faith and fervour for it. I should be distressed that I drop off to sleep during my prayers and during my thanks-giving after Holy Communion. But I don't feel at all distressed. I know that children are just as dear to their parents whether they are asleep or awake and I know that doctors put their patients to sleep before they operate. So I just think that God "knoweth our frame. He remembereth that we are dust."

So this retreat before my Profession was quite barren—like those afterwards. Yet, even though I didn't realise it, I was then being clearly shown how to please God and be good. I have often noticed that Jesus will never give me a store of provisions. He supplies me continually with fresh food and I find myself fed without knowing how. I believe quite simply that it is Jesus Himself, hidden deep in my poor little heart, who works within me in a mysterious manner and inspires all my daily actions.

An hour or two before my Profession I received from Rome, through Father Simeon, the blessing of the Holy Father—a precious blessing which undoubtedly enabled me to weather the most furious storm of my life. The day before Profession is usually such a happy one, but for me it was a day on which my vocation suddenly seemed as unreal as a dream. The devil—for it was he—persuaded me that life in Carmel was quite unsuitable for me and that I was deceiving my superiors in entering a way of life to which I had not been called. My distress was so great that I knew one thing and one thing only: I had no vocation and must go back into the world.

I can't describe what agony I suffered. What was I to do? I did the best thing possible—to tell our novice mistress at once of this temptation. I asked her to come from the choir and, greatly embarrassed, told her of my spiritual condition. Fortunately she saw things much more clearly than I did and laughed at my fears and completely reassured me. The humiliation I felt at telling her all this drove off the devil like magic, for he wanted me to keep quiet about my distress and so remain entangled in his snare. But I was the one who trapped him, for, to complete my humiliation, I also told the whole story to the prioress and her comforting reply blew away the last of my doubts.

On the morning of September 8 peace swept over me and I made my vows in that "peace which surpasseth all understanding." I demanded innumerable favours. I felt that I was really a queen and I made full use of my title to ask the King for every kind of benefit for His ungrateful subjects. I forgot no one. I wanted every sinner to be converted that day and for purgatory to be emptied. Next to my heart I carried this letter saying what I wanted for myself: "O Jesus, let my baptismal robe remain for ever white. Take me, rather than let me stain my soul by the slightest deliberate fault. Let me neither look for nor find anyone but You and You alone. Let all creatures be as nothing to me and me as nothing to them. Let no earthly things disturb my peace. O Jesus, I ask only for peace— peace and above all LOVE that is without measure or limits. May I die as a martyr for You. Give me martyrdom of soul or body. Ah! rather give me both! Enable me to fulfil all my duties perfectly and let me be ignored, trodden underfoot, and forgotten like a grain of sand. To You, my Beloved, I offer myself so that You may fulfill in me Your holy Will without a single creature placing any obstacle in the way."

At the close of that lovely day there was no sadness in my heart as I followed the custom of laying my crown of roses at the foot of the Blessed Virgin's statue, and I felt that time would never dim my joy. How wonderful it was to become the bride of Jesus on the feast of the Nativity of Jesus. It was the little newborn Virgin who presented her *little* flower to the *little* Jesus. Everything was *little* on that day except for the graces I received and the joyful peace I felt as I gazed at the stars in the evening sky and thought that I should soon ascend to heaven and be united with my divine Spouse in eternal happiness.

On September 24 I took the veil. It was a sad day: Daddy was too ill to come and bless his queen, the Bishop could not be there, and there were several other circumstances which cast a veil of sorrow over everything. . . . Yet I found abundant peace at the bottom of the chalice. Jesus did not check my tears, and no one understood why I cried, for I had been dry-eyed during much greater trials. But then I had been helped by grace and on this day Jesus left me to my own resources and my tears showed how feeble they were.

Eight days after I took the veil, our cousin, Jeanne Guérin, married Doctor La Néele. Some time later, as we were talking in the parlour, she told me of all the care she lavished on her husband. Her words stirred me and I said to myself: "It's not going to be said that a woman will do more for her husband, a mere mortal, than I will do for my beloved Jesus." I was filled with fresh ardour and made greater efforts than ever to see that all I did was pleasing to the King of kings who had chosen me as His bride.

When I saw the letter announcing Jeanne's marriage, I amused myself by composing an invitation which I read to the novices to make them realise what had struck me so forcibly: how trifling are the pleasures of an earthly union compared with the glory of being the bride of Jesus.

ALMIGHTY GOD
Creator of Heaven and Earth
Supreme Sovereign of the Universe
and

THE MOST GLORIOUS VIRGIN MARY
Queen of the Court of Heaven

Announce to you the Spiritual Marriage of their august Son

JESUS

KING OF KINGS *and* LORD OF LORDS

with

Little Thérèse Martin

now Princess and Lady of the Kingdoms of the Childhood of Jesus and His Passion, given to her as a dowry by her divine Spouse from which she holds her titles of nobility OF THE CHILD JESUS *and* OF THE HOLY FACE.

It was not possible to invite you to the wedding feast held on the Mountain of Carmel, September 8, 1890, as only the heavenly Court was admitted, but you are nevertheless invited to the At Home tomorrow, the Day of Eternity when Jesus, the Son of God, will come in the clouds of heaven to judge the living and the dead in the full splendour of His majesty.

The hour being uncertain, you are asked to hold yourself in readiness and to watch.

Great graces were given me during the general retreat in the year after my Profession. I usually find preached retreats most trying, but this time it was quite different. I thought I was going to suffer a great deal, so I prepared myself by a fervent novena. The priest who gave the retreat was said to be more concerned with converting sinners than directing nuns. I must have been a great sinner, for God used this priest to help me. I'd all kinds of spiritual troubles then which I had felt incapable of talking about, but I suddenly found I could express myself. The priest was wonderfully understanding and divined what I was getting at. He launched me full sail on the tide of confidence and love which attracted me so much, but upon which I had not dared to venture. He told me my faults did not distress God and said: "I now stand in His place as far as you're concerned and I tell you, as from Him, that He is very pleased with the state of your soul."

I was tremendously happy at hearing such consoling words. I'd never before heard it said that one's faults did not distress God, and I was overwhelmed with joy at this assurance. It gave me patience to endure this life of exile. It was, too, the echo of my own inmost thoughts. For a long time I had realised that Our Lord was more tender than a mother—and how well I know the depths of tenderness in more than one mother's heart! I know that a mother is always ready to forgive the unintentional misbehaviour of her child. I've experienced that so many times myself: a single hug from you moved me far more than any reprimand. With my temperament, fear makes me shrink back, but love makes me come forward—or rather, I fly!

Two months after this retreat our revered foundress, Mother Geneviève of Saint Teresa, left our little Carmel for the Carmel of heaven. Before I go on to tell you, Mother, of what I felt at the moment of her death, I want to say how happy I am at having lived several years alongside a saint whose simple, hidden virtues I could imitate. I've received great consolation from her more than once. One Sunday, when I went to visit her in the infirmary, there were two old sisters with her. I was going to go away, but she called me to her and, as if inspired, said: "Wait a moment, my child. There's just a word I must say to you. You are always asking me for advice on spiritual matters, so now I give you this: Serve God in peace and joy, and never forget that our God is the God of peace." I thanked her and went out, so moved that I wept. I was certain that God had shown her the state of my soul, for I had been most sad and disturbed that day and wrapped in such spiritual darkness that I no longer knew if God loved me. You can guess how the joy and comfort of those words swept away the shadows.

Next Sunday I asked Mother Geneviève if she had had any revelation about me. She assured me she had not, and my admiration
was even greater, for I realised to what a remarkable extent Jesus
dwelt in her soul and inspired her words and deeds. That kind of
sanctity strikes me as the truest, the holiest. It is the sort I want, for
it is free of all illusions.

I was granted a very special grace on the day she died. It was
the first time I'd seen anyone die and it was a most inspiring sight.
Yet a kind of numbness gripped me during the two hours I spent at
the foot of her bed. But at the exact moment when she entered
heaven, my feelings changed completely. In a flash I was filled with
an indescribable joy, just as if the radiant soul of our holy Mother
had given me, at that instant, a bit of the bliss she was already enjoying, for I'm quite convinced she went straight to heaven.

I once said to her: "Oh, Mother, you won't go to purgatory." "I
hope not," she said quietly. And indeed all the favours we have had
since her death prove that God could not betray a hope expressed
with such humility.

Every sister hastened to seize a relic of our mother and you
know the one I keep so carefully. During her last agony I noticed a
tear shining on an eyelash like a lovely diamond. It stayed there, the
last of all she had shed on earth, and I saw it still glittering when her
body was placed in the choir. In the evening I took a scrap of linen
and went to her without anyone seeing me. And now I possess a
saint's last tear.

I don't believe my dreams have any importance. They are
rarely symbolic and I ask myself why, as I think about God all day
long, I don't dream more about Him when I'm asleep. Uusually I
dream about woods and flowers, streams and the sea. I nearly always see pretty little children and catch birds and butterflies unlike
any I've ever seen. So you see, Mother, there is nothing mystical

about my dreams, however poetic they are. But one night after the death of Mother Geneviève I had a more comforting dream. In it I saw her and she gave each of us something which had belonged to her. Her hands were empty when my turn came and I thought I should get nothing. She looked at me tenderly and said three times: "To you, I leave my heart."

Towards the end of 1891, a month after Mother Geneviève's death, an influenza epidemic raged through the community. I had only a slight attack and, with two other sisters, was able to get about. Carmel was in a heartbreaking state during those melancholy days. Those who were really seriously ill were looked after by nuns who could hardly walk. Death was everywhere, and as soon as one sister died, we had to leave her at once to attend to another. My nineteenth birthday was saddened by the death of the subprioress. Along with the nun in charge of the infirmary, I helped at her death agony. Two more deaths followed quickly. I had no one to help me in the sacristy and I don't know how I was able to manage. One morning, as I was getting up, I had the feeling that Sister Madeleine was dead. The corridor was pitch dark and no one had come out of her cell. I went into Sister Madeleine's. She was lying on her mattress, dressed but in the stillness of death. I wasn't afraid. I hurried to the sacristy, brought back a candle, and placed a crown of roses on her head. In the midst of all this desolation I felt the hand of God and knew that He watched over us. Our sisters passed easily into a better life; a heavenly joy shone from their faces and they seemed to lie in a gentle sleep.

During three long weeks of trial I was able to have the tremendous consolation of daily Holy Communion. How sweet it was! Jesus spoilt me for a long time, much longer than He did His more faithful brides, for, after the influenza had gone, He came to me daily for several more months and the rest of the community didn't share this joy. I had not asked for any special treatment, but I was most happy to be united each day with my Beloved. I was also allowed to handle the sacred vessels and to prepare the altar linen which was to receive Jesus. I felt that I must be very fervent and I often recalled the words addressed to a deacon: "Be holy, you who carry the vessels of the Lord."

What can I tell you, Mother, of my thanksgiving after Holy Communion—both at that time and always? I have less consolation then than I ever have! And it's very natural, for I don't want Our Lord to visit me for my own satisfaction, but only for His pleasure.

I picture my soul as a patch of bare ground and I beg the Blessed Virgin to clear it of all rubbish (my imperfections) and then build there a vast pavilion fit for heaven and adorn it with her own jewels. Then I invite all the angels and saints to come and sing hymns of love. It seems to me that Jesus is pleased to see Himself received with such magnificence. I share His delight. But it doesn't prevent me from being distracted and feeling sleepy. So I often resolve to continue my thanksgiving throughout the whole day, as I've made it so badly in choir.

So you see, darling Mother, that the path I tread is far from the way of fear. I always know how to be happy in spite of my failings and to profit from them. Our Lord Himself encourages me along this path. Once—and it was unusual—I felt worried at the thought of approaching the altar. For several days there had not been enough Hosts and I had been given only part of one. That morning I foolishly thought: "If I receive only half a Host today, I shall know that Jesus comes to me reluctantly." I went up and, to my joy, the priest paused and then gave me *two separate Hosts!* Wasn't that a gracious reply?

O Mother, I have so many reasons for being grateful to God! I'm going to make a very ingenuous confession: God has shown the same mercy to me as to King Solomon. All my desires have been fulfilled. I don't mean only my desires for perfection, but also for those things I knew were worthless, even though I hadn't experienced them. I had always had you as my ideal and wanted to be like you in everything. I saw you paint charming miniatures and write beautiful poetry, and I thought how happy I should be if I too could paint, write poetry, and help those around me. But I would never have asked for these natural gifts and my longing stayed hidden in my heart. Jesus, who was also hidden in my poor little heart, showed me once again the vanity of earthly things. I astonished the community by painting several pictures, writing some poetry, and by helping a few souls. And like Solomon, who when he "turned to all the works which his hands had wrought and to the labours wherein he had laboured in vain, saw in all things vanity and vexation of mind," experience taught me that the only way to get happiness in this world is to hide oneself away and remain in ignorance of all created things. I know that without love all we do is worthless. So instead of harming my soul, the talents God bestowed on me drew me closer to Him. I saw that He alone was unchanging and that He alone could satisfy the immensity of my desires.

Since I'm talking about my desires, there's a quite different one that Our Lord granted me. It was a childish one, like my longing for snow when I was clothed. You know, Mother, how I adore flowers. By entering Carmel at fifteen, I had renounced for good the joy of wandering through fields gay with spring flowers. Yet I've never had more flowers than since I came to Carmel. Outside in the world young men give their sweethearts pretty nosegays of flowers. Jesus did not forget this. To adorn His altar I received masses of my favourite flowers—cornflowers, poppies, and marguerites. Only one little friend was missing—the corn-cockle. I longed to see it again and now, only recently, I saw it smiling at me and showing me that in small things as in big, God gives a hundredfold, even in this life, to those who have left all for love of Him.

I still wanted one thing: that Céline would enter the Carmel of Lisieux. It was my dearest wish and one that, for many reasons, was most unlikely to be realised. However, I sacrificed my own wishes and put my darling sister's future into God's hands. I was resigned to her going to the other side of the world if she had to, but I wanted her to be, like me, the bride of Jesus. I suffered a lot at the thought of her in the world and exposed to dangers I had never known. My sisterly affection for her was more like a mother's love. I was devoted to her and full of uneasiness about the state of her soul. One day she had to go to a party with my aunt and cousins. I don't know why I felt more upset than ever about this, but I cried and cried and begged Our Lord to stop her dancing. And that is exactly what He did. He did not allow her to dance that evening, although usually she danced well. Her partner found himself unable to dance. To everyone's amazement all he could do was to walk solemnly around with her. The moment the dance was over, the wretched young man vanished, looking very ashamed, and dared not appear again the whole evening. This happening increased my confidence and showed me plainly that Jesus had set His mark on the forehead of my beloved sister.

On July 29 last year God took to Himself our sorely tried and saintly father. For the two years before his death Uncle looked after him with every possible care. But because he was so ill and weak, we saw him only once in the parlour throughout his illness. What a meeting that was! I know how well you remember it, Mother. When the time came for us to part and we told him we would see him again, he looked upwards and pointed to the sky. He stayed like that for several moments and could make his meaning clear only by uttering the words "in heaven" in a voice choked with tears.

When he went to heaven, the bonds holding his "consoling angel" in the world were snapped. But angels do not stay on earth. Once they have finished their job, they return to God. That's why they have wings! And so Céline tried to fly to Carmel. But the obstacles seemed insurmountable. When the whole affair was getting more and more entangled, I said to Our Lord after Holy Communion: "You know, Jesus, that I wanted my father's sufferings here to replace purgatory for him. And now I long to know if my prayers have been answered. I am not asking You to speak to me. I ask only for a sign. You know that Sister X is opposed to Céline's entry. If she now drops her opposition, that will be Your answer and You will have told me that Father has gone straight to heaven." How infinite is the gracious mercy of God! He, who holds in His hand the hearts of His creatures and moulds them as He wills, altered the feelings of this sister. She was the first person I met immediately after my thanksgiving. Tears were in her eyes as she spoke to me about Céline's entry and she showed a keen longing for her to be with us. The Bishop very soon swept away the final obstacles and without the slightest hesitation allowed you, Mother, to open our doors to the little exiled dove.

Now I wish for only one thing—to love Jesus even unto folly! Love alone attracts me. I no longer wish for either suffering or death and yet both are precious to me. For a long time I've hailed them as messengers of joy. I've already known suffering and I've thought I was approaching the eternal shore. From my earliest days I have believed that the Little Flower would be plucked in the springtime of her life. But today my only guide is self-abandonment. I have no other compass. I no longer know how to ask passionately for anything except that the will of God shall be perfectly accomplished in my soul. I can repeat these words of our Father, St. John of the Cross: "I drank deep within the hidden cellar of my

Beloved and, when I came forth again, I remembered nothing of the flock I used to look after. My soul is content to serve Him with all its strength. I've finished all other work except that of love. In that is all my delight."

Or rather: "Love has so worked within me that it has transformed my soul into itself."

O Mother, how sweet is the way of love! Of course one may stumble and be guilty of small faults, but love, able to draw good from everything, will very quickly destroy all that displeases Jesus and will fill one's heart with a deep and humble peace.

I have had great enlightenment from the writings of St. John of the Cross. When I was between seventeen and eighteen, they were my only spiritual food. But as I grew older, religious writers left me quite unmoved. I'm still like that. If I glance at a book, no matter how good and moving it is, my heart at once contracts and I read without understanding or, if I understand, I cannot meditate on it. When I'm in this state, the Bible and *The Imitation* come to my rescue. In them I find hidden manna, a pure and substantial food. But, above all, the Gospels help me in my prayers. They are always showing me new ways of looking at things, and I am always finding hidden and mysterious meanings in them. I understand and, by experience, I know that the Kingdom of God is within us. Jesus has no need of books or doctors of the Church to guide souls. He, the Doctor of doctors, can teach without words. I have never heard Him speak, but I know that He is within me. He guides and inspires me every moment of the day. Just when I need it, a new light shines on my problems. This happens not so much during my hours of prayer as when I'm busy with my daily work.

With so many graces can I not sing with the Psalmist that "the Lord is good, that His mercy endureth for ever"? I think that if everyone received the favours that I have had, no one would fear

God but would love Him to excess. And because of this love, rather than from any fear, no one would ever willingly be guilty of the slightest fault.

I know that every soul cannot be alike. There must be different kinds so that each of the perfections of God can be specially honoured. To me, He has revealed His infinite mercy, and I see all His other attributes in the light of that. Thus they all seem glowing with love: His justice, perhaps even more than the others, is clothed with love, for how sweet a joy it is to think that God is just; that, in other words, He makes allowances for our weaknesses and understands perfectly the frailty of our humanity. So what have I to be afraid of? If God, who is perfectly just, shows such mercy in forgiving the prodigal son, must He not also be *just* to me "who am always with Him"?

In 1895 I was enabled to understand more clearly than ever before how Jesus longs to be loved. I was thinking of those souls who offer themselves as victims to the justice of God, so that, by drawing it down on themselves, they turn aside the punishment due to sinners. I thought this a noble and generous offer, but I was a long way from feeling that I should make it myself. From the depths of my heart, I cried: "O my divine Master, must it be only Your justice which has its victims? Hasn't Your merciful love need of them too? It is everywhere rejected and ignored. Those on whom You long to lavish it seek a wretched, fleeting happiness in other creatures instead of flinging themselves into Your arms and welcoming the flames of Your divine love. Must Your rejected love stay shut up in Your Heart? It seems to me that if You found souls offering themselves as sacrificial victims of Your love, You would consume them speedily and would rejoice to unloose those torrents of infinite tenderness You hold within Yourself. If Your justice must spend itself, though it is concerned only with the earth, how much more must

Your merciful love long to inflame souls since 'Thy mercy reacheth even to the heavens.' O Jesus, let me be Your eager victim and consume Your little sacrifice in the fire of divine love."

You, Mother, let me make this offering of myself to God, and you know what flames—or rather what oceans of grace—flooded my soul immediately after I gave myself on June 9, 1895. Ah, since that day I have been soaked and engulfed in love. There is not a second when this merciful love does not renew and cleanse me, sweeping every trace of sin from my heart. It's impossible for me to fear purgatory. I know I do not deserve even to enter that place of expiation, but I know also that the fire of love cleanses more than the flames of purgatory. I know too that Jesus does not want us to suffer uselessly, and that He would not inspire me with such desires unless He meant to fulfil them. And that, my beloved Mother, is all I can tell you of the life of your little Thérèse. You know much better than she does just what she is and what Jesus has done for her, and so you'll forgive me for having shortened the story of her religious life a good deal.

How will this "story of a little white flower" end? Perhaps the Little Flower will be gathered in her freshness or transplanted to some other shore. I don't know, but what I am sure of is this: the mercy of God will be with her always and she will never cease to bless the mother who gave her to Jesus. For all eternity she will rejoice to be one of the flowers in her crown, and for all eternity she will sing with her that hymn of love and gratitude which is always new.

CHAPTER NINE

You, Reverend Mother, have said that I should write—for you—the end of my hymn to the mercies of the Lord. I do not want to argue, but I must smile as I pick up my pen to tell you of things you know as well as I do. Yet I obey you. I will not ask what can be the use of this manuscript. And I assure you that I should not be a bit upset if you burnt it in front of me without troubling to read it.

The nuns think that you have spoilt me in every possible way from the very moment I entered Carmel, but "man seeth those things that appear, but the Lord beholdeth the heart." I thank you for not having spared me. Jesus knew very well that His little flower needed the life-giving water of humiliation. She was not strong enough to take root without it, and she owes that priceless favour to you.

For several months Jesus has completely changed His method of cultivating His little flower. He found, no doubt, that she had had enough of that bitter water, so now He sees to it that she grows beneath the warmth of a genial sun. Now He gives her only smiles—something entirely owing to you, Reverend Mother. This sun never withers the Little Flower. It makes her grow wonderfully. Deep within her petals she treasures the precious drops of dew she received in days gone by. They always remind her how small and weak she is. Everyone can stoop down over her, admire her, and shower flattery on her, but it won't give her a scrap of that foolish self-satisfaction which would spoil the real happiness she has in knowing that is nothing but a poor little nonentity in God's eyes. When I say that all praise leaves me unmoved, I'm not thinking of the love and confidence you show me. I'm very moved by it, but I feel that I now need have no fear of praise and that I can accept it calmly. For I attribute to God all the goodness with which He has endowed me. It is nothing to do with me if it pleases Him to make me seem better than I am. He is free to do what He wants.

How different, Lord, are the paths along which You guide souls! In the lives of the saints we find many who left nothing behind them, not the smallest souvenir or a scrap of writing. But there are others, like our Mother St. Teresa, who have enriched the Church by their teaching. They were not afraid to reveal "the secrets of the King," so that souls, by knowing Him better, would love Him more. Which kind of life is most pleasing to Our Lord? I think both are equally acceptable. All those loved by God have followed the prompting of the Holy Ghost, who made the prophet write: "Tell the just man that all is well." Yes, all is well when one tries to do nothing but God's will, and that is why I obey Jesus by trying to please you who are to me His representative on earth.

You know, Mother, that I have always wanted to become a saint. Unfortunately when I have compared myself with the saints, I have always found that there is the same difference between the saints and me as there is between a mountain whose summit is lost in the clouds and a humble grain of sand trodden underfoot by passers-by. Instead of being discouraged, I told myself: God would not make me wish for something impossible and so, in spite of my little-ness, I can aim at being a saint. It is impossible for me to grow big-ger, so I put up with myself as I am, with all my countless faults. But I will look for some means of going to heaven by a little way which is very short and very straight, a little way that is quite new. We live in an age of inventions. We need no longer climb labori-ously up flights of stairs; in well-to-do houses there are lifts. And I was determined to find a lift to carry me to Jesus, for I was far too small to climb the steep stairs of perfection. So I sought in Holy Scripture some idea of what this lift I wanted would be, and I read these words from the very mouth of eternal Wisdom: "Whosoever is a little one, let him come to me." I drew nearer to God, fully real-ising that I had found what I was looking for. I also wanted to know how God would deal with a "little one," so I continued my search and found this: "You shall be carried at the breasts and upon the knees; as one whom the mother caresseth, so will I comfort you." Never before had I been gladdened by such sweet and tender words. It is Your arms, Jesus, which are the lift to carry me to heaven. And so there is no need for me to grow up. In fact, just the opposite: I must stay little and become less and less. O God, You have gone beyond anything I hoped for and I will sing of Your mercies: "Thou hast taught me, O Lord, from my youth, and till now I have declared Thy wonderful works and shall do so unto old age and grey hairs."

When shall I reach old age? It seems to me that it may just as well be now as later, for two thousand years are no more than twenty in God's sight—or than a single day!

But you must not believe, Mother, that your child wishes to leave you, Mother, because she considers it a greater grace to die in the morning of her life rather than at the close of day. What she values and all she longs for is to give Jesus pleasure. Her heart rejoices now that He seems to be coming near to take her to heaven, for she knows and fully understands that God needs no one—her least of all—to do good on earth.

Whilst I wait, Reverend Mother, I know what you want: you want me to carry out at your side an easy and pleasant task and one which I shall finish from heaven. You told me, as Jesus told St. Peter: "Feed my lambs." I was astonished, for I thought myself too insignificant, and I begged you to feed your lambs yourself and to take care of me along with them. You yielded a little to my request by making me the senior novice rather than novice mistress. Yet you have ordered me to lead them to fertile and shady pastures, to point out to them the best and most nourishing grass and to warn them of those bright-hued but poisonous flowers which they must never touch except to crush them underfoot.

Have you never been frightened, Mother, by my youth and inexperience? Why have you no fear that I shall let your lambs stray? But perhaps you remembered that God often likes to bestow wisdom on babes and sucklings.

Most people judge God's power by their own limited understanding. They readily admit that there are exceptions, but God alone is denied the right to make them. I know human beings always measure experience by age. In his youth David sang to the

Lord: "I am young and despised," yet at the same time he is not afraid to say: "I have had understanding above old men, because I have sought Thy commandments; Thy word is a lamp to my feet and a light to my paths; I have sworn and I am determined to keep the judgements of Thy justice."

You did not even consider it ill advised, Mother, to tell me one day that Our Lord was enlightening me and giving me the experience of years. Now I'm too little to have any vanity and I'm too little to know how to spin fine words to try to make it appear how extremely humble I am. I prefer to acknowledge simply that "He that is mighty hath done great things to me," and the greatest thing is to have shown me my littleness and my inability to do anything good.

My soul has known many trials and I have suffered a great deal. When I was a child, I was sad when I suffered, but now I relish every bitter fruit with peace and joy. Dear Mother, if you are not to smile as you read these pages, you have, I admit, to know me inside out, for is there anyone who seems to have suffered less? How astonished everyone would be if the martyrdom I have endured for the past year became known. As you want me to, I shall describe it, but words are quite inadequate to express such things and whatever I write will always fall short of the reality.

In Lent last year I felt stronger than ever and kept perfectly healthy until Holy Week—in spite of the fasting which I observed in all its strictness. But during the first hour of Good Friday Jesus roused my hopes of soon going to join Him in heaven. How wonderful the memory of it is! On Thursday I went to my cell at midnight, as I had been refused permission to stay by the Altar of Repose throughout the night. I had scarcely put my head on the pillow when a warm gush of something filled my mouth. I thought I was dying and my heart almost burst with joy. But as I had just put out my lamp, I restrained my curiosity until morning and went peacefully to sleep. When the bell for getting up rang at five o'clock, I remembered at once that I'd some good news to check. I went to the window and saw the good news was true—my handkerchief was sodden with blood. What hope I had, Mother! I was absolutely sure that, on this anniversary of His death, my Beloved had let me hear His first call, like a gentle, far-off murmur which heralded His joyful arrival.

I assisted at Prime and Chapter with great fervour and rushed to kneel before you and tell you of my happiness. I felt not the least bit tired nor had I the slightest pain, and so I easily got permission to finish Lent as I had begun. On that Good Friday I shared to the full all the austerities of Carmel and they had never seemed so delightful. The hope of going to heaven transported me with joy.

On the evening of that happy day I went back joyfully to my cell and was going to fall quietly asleep when my dear Jesus gave me, as on the night before, the same sign that I should soon be entering eternal life. In those days my faith was so clear and vigorous that I found perfect happiness in the thought of heaven. I could not believe that there were people without faith and I was convinced they did not mean what they said when they denied the existence of another world. But during those radiant days of Easter Jesus made me realise that there really are people who by the abuse of grace have lost those precious treasures of faith and hope which are the source of the only real and innocent joy. He allowed pitch-black darkness to sweep over my soul and let the thought of heaven, so sweet to me from my infancy, destroy all my peace and torture me. This trial was not something lasting a few days or weeks. I suffered it for months and I am still waiting for it to end. I wish I could express what I feel, but it is impossible. One must have travelled through the same sunless tunnel to understand how dark it is. But I will do my best to explain it.

Imagine that I was born in a country wrapped in a dense fog and that I had never seen the smiling face of nature nor a single ray of sunlight. It is true that from my early childhood I heard these wonders spoken of and I knew that this country where I lived was not my native land, and that there was another I must never cease to long for. This was not a tale invented by another dweller in the fog: it was an undeniable truth, for the King of that sun-bathed land had spent thirty-three years in the land of darkness and "the darkness did not understand that He was the Light of the World." But, Lord, Your child knows that You are the Light. She asks You to forgive her unbelieving brethren; she will willingly eat the bread of sorrow for as long as You wish; she will, for love of You, sit at this table where the wretched sinners eat their bitter food and will not leave it until You give her the sign. But may she not say in her own name and in the name of her guilty brethren: "O God, be merciful to us sinners. Send us away justified! May all those who have never been illumined by the light of faith see it shine at last! O God, if the table defiled by them must be cleansed by one who loves You, I will gladly stay there alone and eat the bread of sorrow until You are pleased to lead me to Your kingdom of light. I ask of You only one favour: that I may never displease You."

I told you, Mother, that I had been certain from childhood that I should one day leave this land of darkness. I believed this not only because of what I was told, but also because, deep down within me, I felt that one day I should dwell for ever in another and more beautiful country. I was like Christopher Columbus whose genius sensed the existence of a new world. Then, quite suddenly, the mists which surrounded me sank into my soul and smothered it so that I could not even picture this lovely country ... everything about it had vanished!

My sufferings increased whenever I grew wearied by the surrounding darkness and tried to find peace and strength by thinking of eternal life. For the voice of unbelievers came to mock me out of the darkness: "You dream of light, of a fragrant land, you dream that their Creator will be yours for ever and you think you will one day leave behind this fog in which you languish. Hope on! Hope on! And look forward to death! But it will give you, not what you hope for, but a still darker night, the night of annihilation!"

Dear Mother, this story of my suffering is as inadequate as an artist's sketch compared with his model, but I do not want to write any more about it lest I should blaspheme. I am afraid I have already said too much. May God forgive me! He knows very well that although I had not the consolation of faith, I forced myself to act as if I had. I have made more acts of faith in the last year than in the whole of my life.

I behaved bravely whenever the devil tried to provoke me. I know it is cowardly to fight a duel, so I turned my back on him and never looked at him face to face. I ran towards Jesus and told Him I was ready to shed my last drop of blood to declare there was a heaven, and that I was well content during my stay on earth never to see with the eyes of the spirit the heaven which awaited me, provided He would open it for the wretched unbelievers. And so, in spite of this trial which robs me of all sense of pleasure, I can still say: "Thou hast given me, O Lord, a delight in Thy doings." For is there any greater joy than to suffer for love of You? The more intense and hidden the suffering is, the more pleasing it is to You. And if—which is impossible—You knew nothing of it, I should still be happy to suffer in the hope that, by my tears, I could prevent or perhaps atone for a single sin against the Faith.

I am sure, Reverend Mother, that you will think I am slightly exaggerating this night of my soul. If you think of the poems I have written this year, I must have seemed overwhelmed with spiritual consolation and like a child for whom the veil of faith is almost torn apart. But there is no veil, but instead a wall which towers to the sky and hides the stars.

When I sing of the bliss of heaven and the eternal possession of God, I get no joy from it, for I am singing only of *what I want to believe*. Sometimes, I admit, a tiny ray of sunshine pierces the darkness and then, for a second, my suffering stops. Instead of comforting me, the memory of this makes the darkness blacker.

I have never before felt so strongly how gentle and merciful God is. He sent me this heavy cross just at the time when I was strong enough to bear it. At any other time it would have disheartened me. Now it has only one result: it removes all natural satisfaction from my longing for heaven.

It seems to me, Mother, that nothing now hinders me from flying there. I no longer want anything except to love until I die of love. I am free and fear nothing. I am not even afraid—and it used to be my greatest fear that my illness will drag out and make me a burden to the community. If it pleases God, I am willing for my suffering, both bodily and spiritual, to last for years. I am not afraid of a long life. I do not refuse the struggle: "The Lord is a rock upon which I stand; He teaches my hands to fight and my fingers to war. He is my protector and I have hoped in Him." I have never asked God to let me die young, but I have always thought He would, even though I have not asked.

God is often content with the mere longing to work for His glory, and you are aware, Mother, of how intense my longing has been. You know too that Jesus has offered me more than one bitter cup in connection with my beloved sisters. David was right when he sang: "Behold how good and how pleasant it is for brethren to dwell together in unity." But on earth this unity can be achieved only by sacrifice. I did not enter Carmel to live with my sisters; on the contrary, I clearly foresaw how much I should suffer when I could not give way to my natural affection for them. I do not understand people saying that it is holier to keep aloof from one's relatives. No one ever blames brothers for fighting side by side on the same battlefield or for winning the palm of martyrdom together. It is quite true they encourage each other, but the sufferings of one hurt all the others. It is exactly the same in life in religion, that life which theologians call a martyrdom. To offer oneself to God does not mean that one loses anything at all of one's natural tenderness. It is just the opposite, for this tenderness deepens as it becomes purified by centering on divine things. It is with this deepened tenderness, Mother, that I love you and my sisters. I am glad to fight as one of a family for the glory of God, but I am also ready to depart to another battlefield if He wishes. No order would be necessary. Just a look or sign would be enough.

Since I entered Carmel, I have thought the fate of Noë's dove would be mine unless Jesus took me to heaven quickly. One day he would open the window of the ark and tell me to fly far away to heathen shores, carrying the olive twig with me. This thought has made me soar above all earthly considerations. I knew that separations were possible even in Carmel, and so I have tried to live in heaven before my time. I accepted the likelihood of my own exile in the midst of an unknown people and, what was far more bitter, a similar exile for my sisters. The Carmel of Saïgon, founded by our Carmel, asked for two of them, and for a time there was serious thought of sending them. I refused to say a word to hold them back, although my heart ached at the thought of the difficulties awaiting them. Now all that is over. The superiors have put insurmountable obstacles in their way. So I have only touched this chalice with my lips—just enough to taste its bitterness.

If the Blessed Virgin cures me, I want to answer the appeal of our community in Hanoï. To live in foreign Carmels needs a very special vocation, and many think they are called who are not. But you have told me, Mother, that I have this vocation and that only my health stands in the way. I should suffer terribly if I had ever to leave here. My heart is far from hard, and it is because it can suffer so much that I want to offer Jesus all it is able to endure. You love me, Mother, and so do all the other nuns. This love is very precious to me, and that is why I dream of a convent where I should be unknown and forced to endure the pain of exile. There my only aim would be to do the will of God and to welcome every sacrifice He wished. I know I should not be disappointed, for the slightest pleasure is a surprise when one expects nothing but suffering. And suffering itself becomes the greatest of all joys when one seeks it like a precious treasure.

But now I am ill and I shall not get better. Yet I am at peace. For a long time I have not belonged to myself, but have completely abandoned myself to Jesus. . . . So He is free to do whatever He wants with me. He gave the desire for exile and asked if I would drink from that chalice. I tried at once to grasp it, but He withdrew it, satisfied with my willingness.

O God, from what trouble are we freed by the vow of obedience! How happy simple nuns are! The will of their superiors is their only compass and so they are always certain of travelling in the right direction. They can never feel mistaken, even if they are certain their superiors are wrong. If, though, one stops being guided by this compass for a single moment, the soul strays into a desert where the waters of grace quickly fail. You, Mother, are the compass Jesus has given me to guide me surely to the eternal shore.

It gives me such delight to gaze at you and so fulfil the will of God. By letting my faith be tempted, God has greatly increased my *spirit of faith* which makes me see Him living in your soul and giving me, through you, His commands. I know very well, Mother, that you make the burden of obedience light and pleasant, but I am just as well aware that my behaviour would be the same and my love for you would remain unchanged if you treated me harshly. For I should still see in your attitude the will of God manifesting itself for the good of my soul.

Among the countless graces I have received this year, perhaps the greatest has been that of being able to grasp in all its fulness the meaning of charity. I had never before fathomed Our Lord's words: "The second commandment is like to the first: Thou shalt love thy neighbour as thyself." I had striven above all to love God, and in loving Him I discovered the secret of those other words: "Not everyone that saith to me: Lord, Lord! shall enter into the kingdom of heaven, but he that doeth the will of my Father." Jesus made me understand what this will was by the words He used at the Last Supper when He gave His "new commandment" and told His apostles "to love one another as He had loved them." I began to consider just how Jesus had loved His disciples. I saw it was not for their natural qualities, for I recognised they were ignorant men and often preoccupied with earthly affairs. Yet He calls them His friends and His brethren. He wants to see them near Him in the kingdom of His Father and to open this kingdom to them He wills to die on the Cross, saying: "Greater love than this no man hath, that a man lay down his life for his friends." As I meditated on these words of Jesus, I saw how imperfect was my love for the other nuns and I knew that I did not love them as Jesus loves them. But now I realise that true charity consists in putting up with all one's neighbour's faults, never being surprised by his weakness, and being inspired by the least of his virtues. Above all, I learnt that charity is not something that stays shut up in one's heart for "no man lighteth a candle and putteth it in a hidden place, nor under a bushel; but upon a candlestick, that they who come in may see the light." This candle represents that charity which must illumine and cheer not only those dearest to me but "All those who are of the household."

When God, under the old law, told His people to love their neighbours as themselves, He had not yet come down to earth. As He knew how much we love ourselves, He could not ask us to do more. But when Jesus gave His apostles a "new commandment, His own commandment," He did not ask only that we should love our neighbours as ourselves but that we should love them as He loves them and as He will love them to the end of time. O Jesus, I know You command nothing that is impossible. You know how weak and imperfect I am, and You know only too well that I could never love the other nuns as You love them if You Yourself did not love them *within me*. It is because You wish to grant me this grace that You have given a new commandment. How I cherish it, for it assures me that it is Your will *to love in me* all those whom You command me to love.

When I act and think with charity, I feel it is Jesus who works within me. The closer I am united with Him, the more I love all the other dwellers in Carmel. If I want this love to grow deeper and the devil tries to show me the faults of a sister, I hasten to think of all her virtues and of how good her intentions are. I tell myself that though I have seen her commit a sin, she may very well have won many spiritual victories of which I know nothing because of her humility. What seems a fault to me may very well be an act of virtue because of the intention behind it. I have experienced that myself. During recreation one day the portress came to ask for a sister to help her with a certain job. I wanted to take a hand in that particular bit of work and sure enough I was chosen. I at once began to fold up my sewing, but I was slow about it so that the nun next to me was able to fold hers before me, for I knew how pleased she would be to take my place. When she saw me in so little of a hurry, the portress said with a smile: "Ah! I felt sure you would not add this pearl to your crown. You are too slow." And the whole community thought this slowness was natural. I benefitted tremendously from this little incident. It has made me very understanding. It still stops my having any feeling of pride when people think well of what I do, for I say to myself: Since any small good deed I do can be mistaken for a fault, the mistake of calling a fault a virtue can be made just as easily. Then I say with St. Paul: "To me it is a very small thing to be judged by you, or by man's day. But neither do I judge myself. He that judgeth me is the Lord." As it is Jesus who judges me, and as He said: "Judge not and ye shall not be judged," I want always to have charitable thoughts so that He will judge me favourably—or, rather, not judge me at all.

To return to the Gospels where Our Lord teaches me so clearly what His new commandment is. In St. Matthew I read: "You have heard that it hath been said, Thou shall love thy neighbour and hate thy enemy: but I say unto you, love your enemies and pray for them that persecute you." In Carmel, of course, one has no enemies, but one certainly has natural likes and dislikes. One feels attracted to a certain sister and one would go out of one's way to dodge meeting another. Jesus tells me that it is this very sister I must love, and I must pray for her even though her attitude makes me believe she has no love for me. "If you love them that love you, what thanks are to you? For sinners also love those that love them." It is not enough to love. We must prove that we do. We naturally like to please a friend, but that is not charity, for so do sinners.

Jesus also teaches me: "Give to everyone that asketh thee; and of him that taketh away thy goods, ask them not again." It is not so pleasant to give to everyone who asks as it is to offer something freely and spontaneously; and it is easy to give when you are asked nicely, but if we are asked tactlessly, we at once want to refuse unless perfect charity strengthens us. We find a thousand reasons for saying no, and it is not until we have made the sister aware of her bad manners that we give her what she wants *as a favour,* or do her a slight service which takes a quarter of the time needed to tell her of the obstacles preventing our doing it or of our fancied rights.

If it is hard to give to anyone who asks, it is very much harder to let what belongs to us be taken without asking for it back. I say that it is hard, but I should really say that it *seems* hard, for "the yoke of the Lord is sweet and His burden light." The moment we accept it, we feel how light it is.

I have said that Jesus does not want me to ask for the return of what belongs to me. That seems very right, as nothing really does belong to me. So I should rejoice when I have the chance of experiencing that poverty to which I am solemnly vowed. I used to believe I had no possessiveness about anything; but since I have really grasped what Jesus means, I see how far I am from being perfect. If, for example, I settle down to start painting and find the brushes in a mess, or a ruler or a penknife gone, I very nearly lose my patience and have to hold on to it with both hands to prevent my asking bad-temperedly for them. Of course I can ask for these essential tools and I do not disobey Jesus if I ask *humbly.* I behave like poor people who hold out their hands for the necessities of life. As no one owes them anything, they are never surprised at being rebuffed. What peace pours over the soul once it soars above natural feelings! There is no joy like that known by the truly poor in spirit. Our Lord's counsel is: "If any man take away thy coat, let go thy cloak also unto him," and these poor in spirit are following this counsel when they ask, with detachment, for some necessary thing and it is refused them and an effort is made to snatch away even what they have. To give up one's coat means to renounce one's last rights and to regard oneself as the servant and the slave of others. Without one's cloak, it is much easier to walk and run, and so Jesus adds: "And whosoever will force thee one mile, go with him another two." It is not enough for me to give to all who ask me: I must go beyond what they want. I must show how grateful and honoured I am to serve them and if anything I use is taken away, I must appear glad to be rid of it.

There are times, though, when I cannot always keep strictly to the words of the Gospel. Occasions crop up when I have to refuse something. But when charity is deeply rooted in the soul, it shows outwardly. It is possible to refuse in such a gracious manner that the refusal gives as much pleasure as the gift would have done. It is true that people are less embarrassed at asking from those who always show themselves willing to oblige, but I must not avoid the sisters who ask for things easily on the pretext that I shall have to refuse. Our Lord says: "From him that would borrow of thee turn not away." Nor must I be kind just for appearances sake or in the hope that the sister I oblige will one day do the same for me, for Our Lord also says: "If you lend to them of whom you hope to receive, what thanks are to you? For sinners also lend to sinners for to receive as much. But you, do good and lend, hoping for nothing thereby, and your reward shall be great." And the reward is great indeed, even on earth. It is only the first step which counts along this path. It seems hard to lend "hoping for nothing thereby." One would prefer to give, for something given no longer belongs to one. Someone comes up to you and says very earnestly: "Sister, I need your help for a few hours. But don't worry. Reverend Mother has given me permission and I will repay the time you lend me." But I know very well that this borrowed time will never be given back and I would rather say: "I give it you!" But that would feed my self-love, for it is more generous to give than to lend and it would, as well, make the sister feel that I did not rely on her to repay me.

Oh, how contrary to human nature are the divine teachings! Without the help of grace, it would be impossible not only to follow them but even to understand them.

Dear Mother, I feel that, more than ever, I have expressed myself very badly. I do not know how you can take any interest in reading all these muddled thoughts. But, after all, I am not writing a literary work, and if I have bored you by this homily on charity, you will at least see that your child has given proof of her goodwill.

I am, I confess, far from practising what I know I should, yet the mere desire I have to do so gives me peace. If it happens that I fall and commit a fault against charity, I rise again at once. For some months I have no longer even had to struggle. I can say with our Father St. John of the Cross: "My house is entirely at peace," and I attribute this deep peace to a certain battle which I won. Ever since this victory the hosts of heaven come to my aid, for they cannot bear to see me wounded after I fought so valiantly on the occasion I am going to describe.

Formerly one of our nuns managed to irritate me whatever she did or said. The devil was mixed up in it, for it was certainly he who made me see so many disagreeable traits in her. As I did not want to give way to my natural dislike for her, I told myself that charity should not only be a matter of feeling but should show itself in deeds. So I set myself to do for this sister just what I should have done for someone I loved most dearly. Every time I met her, I prayed for her and offered God all her virtues and her merits. I was sure this would greatly delight Jesus, for every artist likes to have his works praised and the divine Artist of souls is pleased when we do not halt outside the exterior of the sanctuary where He has chosen to dwell but go inside and admire its beauty.

I did not remain content with praying a lot for this nun who caused me so much disturbance. I tried to do as many things for her as I could, and whenever I was tempted to speak unpleasantly to her, I made myself give her a pleasant smile and tried to change the subject. *The Imitation* says: "It is more profitable to leave to everyone his way of thinking than to give way to contentious discourses."

When I was violently tempted by the devil and if I could slip away without her seeing my inner struggle, I would flee like a soldier deserting the battlefield. And after all this she asked me one day with a beaming face: "Sister Thérèse, will you please tell me what attracts you so much to me? You give me such a charming smile whenever we meet." Ah! it was Jesus hidden in the depth of her soul who attracted me, Jesus who makes the bitterest things sweet!

I have just told you, Mother, of my last resolve for avoiding a defeat in the struggles of life—*desertion*. I used this rather dishonourable trick when I was a novice and it was always completely successful. I will give you a striking example which, I think, will make you smile.

You had been ill for some days with bronchitis and we were very worried. One morning I came very guiltily to the infirmary to put back the keys of the Communion grille, for I was sacristan. I was feeling delighted at having this opportunity of seeing you, but I took good care not to let it be seen. One of the sisters, full of zeal, thought I was going to waken you and tried to take the keys quietly from me. I told her, as politely as possible, that I was just as eager as she was to make no noise, and added that it was my duty to return the keys. Nowadays I realise that it would have been far better simply to have given her them, but I did not understand that then and tried to push my way into the room in spite of her.

Then what we feared happened. The noise we made woke you and all the blame fell on me! The sister I had opposed hastened to make quite a speech, the gist of which was: "It was Sister Thérèse of the Child Jesus who made the noise." I burned to defend myself, but fortunately I had a bright idea. I knew, without a shadow of a doubt, that if I began to speak up for myself I should lose my peace of soul; I knew too that I was not virtuous enough to let myself be accused without saying a word, my only hope of safety was to run away. No sooner thought than done: I fled . . . but my heart beat so violently that I could not go far and I sat down on the stairs to enjoy in peace the fruits of my victory. It was undoubtedly a queer kind of courage, but I think it is better not to fight when defeat is certain.

Alas! When I remember my days as a novice, I see how imperfect I was. I laugh now at some of the things I did. How good God is to have lifted up my soul and given it wings! All the nets of the hunters cannot frighten me, for "a net is set in vain before the eyes of them that have wings."

In the days to come it may be that my present state will seem most imperfect, but I am no longer surprised by anything and I feel no distress at seeing my complete helplessness. On the contrary, I glory in it and every day I expect to discover fresh flaws in myself. In fact, this revelation of my nothingness does me much more good than being enlightened on matters of faith.

I remember that "charity covereth a multitude of sins" and I draw from the rich mine opened by the Lord in the Gospels. I ransack the depths of His adorable words and I cry with David: "I have run the way of Thy commandments when Thou didst enlarge my heart." Charity alone can enlarge my heart. . . . O Jesus, ever since its gentle flame has consumed my heart, I have run with delight along the way of Your "new commandment" and I want to continue until that blessed day when, with Your company of virgins, I shall follow You through infinite realms singing your *new canticle*—the canticle of LOVE.

CHAPTER TEN

God has allowed me to explore the hidden
depths of charity. And if, Reverend Mother,
I could express all I know, you would hear
the music of heaven. Unfortunately I stammer like a baby and if I were not strengthened by the words of Jesus, I should be
tempted to ask you to let me be silent. When
He tells me: "Give to everyone that asketh
thee, and of him that taketh away thy goods,
ask them not again," I think He is speaking
not only of our material possessions but also
of our spiritual treasures. By the vow of
poverty I renounced the first and the others
are also lent to me by God. He can take them
from me and I have no right to grumble. Yet
our own thoughts, our own ardent ideas and
feelings seem like a treasure which really belongs to us and which no one has a right to

touch. For instance, if I tell a sister about some enlightenment that came to me in prayer and if she later discloses it as if it were hers, I'm inclined to think she has stolen my property. Or if during recreation one whispers something amusing to her neighbour, and she repeats it aloud without saying where it came from, well, that strikes its author as a theft. She may say nothing of it at the time although she would like to, but at the first opportunity she will delicately let it be known that her ideas have been stolen.

I could not explain these pathetic human failings so well, Mother, if I had not suffered from them myself. I should like to have believed that I alone suffered from them, but I learned a great deal by listening to the temptations which beset the novices. In performing this task you gave me, I was forced to practise what I preached.

Now I can say that I am no more attached to my own ideas or feelings than I am to material possessions. If I think of something and speak about it and the other sisters like the idea, I find it quite natural that they grab it as if it belonged to them, for such a thought is the Holy Ghost's, not mine. St. Paul insists that "without the Spirit of love we cannot call God our Father." So this Spirit is at liberty to make use of me to transmit a worthwhile thought to someone else, and I have no right to consider that such a thought belongs exclusively to me. Besides, although I do not despise those fine thoughts which draw us nearer to God, I have realised for a long time that we must be very careful not to rely too much on them. The noblest inspirations are worthless without good works. It is true that some people can benefit greatly from such inspirations if they are humbly grateful to God for letting them share in the banquet of a privileged soul. But if that privileged soul takes pride in her spiritual wealth and prays like the Pharisee, she is like someone dying with hunger in front of a table heaped with food, whilst her guests tuck in and perhaps glance with envy at the owner of so much.

How true it is that God alone knows the secrets of our hearts! We ourselves are so shortsighted. When we meet someone with a deeper spiritual insight, we think God cares more for them than for us. Yet surely God has the right to make use of one of His creatures to give His other children the food they need. He had this right in the days of Pharaoh, for, in Holy Scripture, He told him: "And therefore have I raised thee, that I may show My power in thee, and My name may be spoken of throughout all the earth." Centuries have passed since He uttered these words and His ways have not changed: He has always used human beings to accomplish His work among souls.

If an artist's canvas could think and speak, it would certainly not complain at being constantly touched and retouched by the brush, for it would know that it owes all its beauty not to the brush but to the artist who guides its strokes. And the brush itself cannot take any credit for the masterpiece it paints, for—again imagining it can think—it knows that artists often use the feeblest and most faulty tools. Reverend Mother, I am a tiny brush whom Jesus has chosen to paint His likeness in the souls you have entrusted to me. An artist has several brushes. He must have at least two. The first and most useful puts in the ground tints and very quickly covers the whole canvas; the other is much smaller and fills in the details. To me, Mother, you are the valuable brush held lovingly in the hand of Jesus when He wishes to accomplish some great work in the souls of poor children; I am the very tiny brush He uses afterwards for the unimportant details.

It was around December 8, 1892, that God took up His little brush for the first time. I shall always remember that period as a time of great graces.

When I entered Carmel, I met in the noviciate a woman eight years my senior, but in spite of the difference in our age a real friendship developed. We were allowed to talk together on spiritual matters in order to encourage a friendship which seemed likely to bear good fruit. I was charmed by my companion's innocence and her frank and open character. On the other hand, Mother, I was amazed to see how different from mine was her affection for you, and there were many other things about her which disturbed me. God had already made me realise that His mercy does not grow weary of waiting for some souls and that He enlightens them only slowly. So I took good care not to anticipate Him.

I was thinking one day about the permission we had to talk together so as "to incite one another to a greater love of our Spouse"—in the words of our Holy Rule. I realised sadly that our discussions were not doing this and I saw that I must no longer be afraid of telling her what I thought, or else of stopping these talks which were just like the gossip of friends out in the world. I begged Our Lord to put gentle but convincing words in my mouth, or rather, to speak through me Himself. He answered my prayer, for "those who look upon Him shall be enlightened" and "to the upright a light is risen in the darkness." I applied the first saying to myself and the second to my companion, for she was truly upright. When the time came for our next talk, my poor little sister saw at once that I had changed and she was blushing as she sat down at my side. I drew her to me and tenderly told her what I thought. I showed her what true love was and made her see that when she loved you with a purely natural love it was herself she was loving. I revealed to her the sacrifices I had been compelled to make in this matter at the start of my life in Carmel, and it was not long before her tears mingled with mine. She admitted most humbly that she had been wrong and recognised that what I said was true. She promised to start a new way of life and asked me to be kind enough always to point out her faults. From that moment our affection was wholly spiritual and the words of the Holy Ghost were fulfilled in us: "A brother that is helped by his brother is like a strong city." You know very well, Mother, that I did not want to turn her from you. All I wanted to teach her was that true love grows by sacrifice and that the more thoroughly the soul rejects natural satisfaction, the stronger and more detached its tenderness becomes.

I remember that when I was a postulant I sometimes longed to seek my own satisfaction and enjoy a little pleasure. This longing was so strong that I was forced to hurry past your cell and to clutch the balustrade to prevent myself turning back. A thousand excuses for seeing you came into my head so that I could justify my natural impulses-excuses like asking your permission for various things. How glad I am now that I crushed such impulses right from the start of my religious life! I am already enjoying the reward promised to those who fight bravely. No longer do I feel that I must refuse to let my heart have any comfort, for my heart is centered on God. . . . Because it has loved only Him, it has gradually developed until it can manifest to those dear to Him a tenderness incomparably deeper than if it had spent itself in selfish, barren love.

I have told you, dear Mother, of the first work Jesus and you deigned to paint with His little brush, but it was only a foreshadowing of the masterpiece you later entrusted to it.

The moment I began to deal with souls I realised instantly that the task was beyond my strength. I put myself quickly in the arms of God and behaved like babies who when frightened bury their heads on their fathers' shoulders. I said: "Lord, You see that I am too little to feed Your children. Put food into my hand if it is through me that You want to give each of them what is good for her. Without leaving Your arms and without even turning my head,

I will distribute Your treasure to all the souls who come to ask me for food. When they like it, I shall know it is You they must thank, but if they complain that what I give them is bitter, I shall not be disturbed and shall try to persuade them that the food comes from You. And I shall take good care that it is all they get."

My task was simplified as soon as I realised I could do nothing by myself. Spiritually I bothered about nothing except uniting myself more and more closely to God. My trust has never been let down. My hand has been full just as often as has been necessary for the nourishment of my sisters' souls. I assure you, Mother, that if I had behaved differently and relied on my own strength I should soon have been forced to give up. I know it seems easy to help souls, to make them love God above all, and to mould them according to His will. But actually, without His help it is easier to make the sun shine at night. One must banish one's own tastes and personal ideas and guide souls along the special way Jesus indicates for them rather than along one's own particular way. But even this is not the supremely difficult thing: what cost me more than anything was having to wage a war to the death against the faults and the slightest imperfections I noticed.

I was going to say unhappily for me, but that would be cowardly, so I will say, instead, happily for my sisters, ever since I placed myself in the arms of Jesus, I have been like the watchman keeping an eye on the enemy from the highest turret of a strong fort. Nothing escapes my gaze and I am often astonished to be able to see so clearly. I can understand now why Jonah fled from before the face of the Lord rather than announce the destruction of Nineveh. I would far sooner endure a thousand reproaches than utter one. Yet I feel it is essential that this duty should upset me, for if I followed my natural inclinations, the erring novice could not understand that she was in the wrong. All she would think would be:

"The sister who is directing me is irritable, and she takes this irritability out on me though I am full of the best intentions."

In this, Mother, it is like everything else: in all I do I have to sacrifice my own feelings. I feel, for instance, that no letter I write will have any good effect unless I write it reluctantly and only from obedience. When I speak to a novice, I ensure that I mortify myself and avoid asking her any questions to satisfy my curiosity. If she starts talking about something interesting but breaks off and goes on to a subject which bores me, I take good care not to bring her back to what she was saying, for one does no good by self-seeking.

I am aware, Mother, that your little lambs find me severe! If they read these lines, they would say that I seem singularly untroubled by having to run after them and show them how they have soiled their lovely fleece or by giving them back the tufts of wool they leave on the thorns along the roadside. But no matter what they say, they know in their heart of hearts that I have a very great love for them. There is no danger that I shall be like "the hireling who seeth the wolf coming and leaveth the sheep and flieth." I am ready to "lay down my life for them" and my love is so disinterested that I do not even want them to know about it. By the grace of God, I have never tried to attract them to me. I knew that my mission was to lead them to God and to you, Mother, whom they must love and respect as God's representative.

I have said that I learned a lot by teaching others. I discovered that every soul has almost the same difficulties and that there is yet a vast difference between individual souls—a difference which means that each one must be dealt with differently. There are some with whom I must make myself small and show myself willing to be humiliated by confessing my own struggles and defeats, for then they themselves easily confess their own faults and are pleased that I understand them through my own experience. To be successful with others, firmness is necessary. I must never go back on what I have said, and to humiliate myself would be regarded as weakness.

God has given me the grace of having no fear of a fight. I will do my duty at any cost. More than once I have been told: "If you want to succeed with me, severity is no use. You will get nowhere unless you are gentle." But I know that no one is a good judge in his own case. If a surgeon performs a painful operation on a child, the child will scream and say that the cure is worse than the disease. But after a few days when he is cured, he is delighted to be able to run about and play. It is exactly the same where souls are concerned. They soon realise that a little bitterness is better than sweetness.

Sometimes the change that comes over a soul from one day to the next is like magic. One novice told me: "You were right to be severe with me yesterday. I was indignant at first, but after I had thought over all you said, I recognised how fair you had been. But when I left your cell, I thought that all was over and said to myself: 'I am going straight to Reverend Mother to tell her that I shall have nothing more to do with Sister Thérèse.' But I soon knew that it was the devil who prompted me. I felt you were praying for me and I calmed down. Light began to dawn and now you must instruct me as you will. That is why I have come back."

I was delighted to be able to follow my inclinations and quickly gave her less bitter spiritual food, but at the same time I saw that I must not go ahead too fast, for a single word out of place could destroy the lovely edifice built with tears. If I was unfortunate enough to say anything at all which seemed to soften the truths I had uttered the previous day, I saw that my little sister tried to take advantage of it. So then I prayed, invoked the Blessed Virgin, and—as always—Jesus was victorious. All my strength lies in prayer and sacrifice. They are my invincible weapons, and I know, by experience, that they can soften the heart much better than words.

Two years ago, during Lent, a novice came to me looking radiantly happy. "Do you know what I dreamt last night?" she asked. "I was with my sister who is very worldly and I longed to withdraw her from all earthly vanities. So I explained to her some lines from one of your poems. I was certain that my words sank deep into her heart and I was overjoyed. I believe that God wants me to give Him this soul. Do you think I should write to her for Easter and tell her my dream and say that Jesus wants her for His spouse?" I told her she had better ask permission to write. As Lent was far from over, you were surprised, Mother, at such an untimely request and, obviously inspired by God, you replied that Carmelites should save souls by prayers rather than by letters. When I heard of your decision, I told the novice: "We have got to get to work and pray hard. How marvellous it would be if we were answered at the end of Lent!" How infinite is God's mercy! *At the end of Lent* another soul consecrated herself to Jesus. It was a true miracle of grace and one brought about by the fervour of a humble novice.

The power of prayer is really tremendous. It makes one like a queen who can approach the king at any time and get whatever she asks for. To be sure of an answer, there is no need to recite from a book a formula composed for the occasion. If there were, I should have to be pitied.

Though I'm quite unworthy, I love to say the Divine Office every day, but apart from that I cannot bring myself to hunt through books for beautiful prayers. There are so many of them that I get a headache. Besides, each prayer seems lovelier than the next. I cannot possibly say them all and do not know which to choose, I behave like children who cannot read: I tell God very simply what I want and He always understands. For me, prayer is an upward leap of the heart, an untroubled glance towards heaven, a cry of gratitude and love which I utter from the depths of sorrow as well as from the heights of joy. It has a supernatural grandeur which expands the soul and unites it with God. I say an Our Father or a Hail Mary when I feel so spiritually barren that I cannot summon up a single worthwhile thought. These two prayers fill me with rapture and feed and satisfy my soul.

But what was I writing about? Once again I am lost in the maze of my thoughts. Forgive me, Mother, for being so confused. I admit that this story is a very tangled skein. Unfortunately I do not know how to do any better: I write just as the ideas come into my head. I sit, as it were, and cast my fishing line at random into the little stream flowing through my heart. Then I offer you my tiny fish just as they are caught.

I was talking about the novices. They often say to me: "You have an answer for everything, but this time I thought I should catch you out. Where do you get the knowledge of the things you teach us?" They are even ingenuous enough to believe that I can read their souls, because I have happened to reveal to them—without having had any revelation—what they were thinking about.

The senior novice was determined to hide from me a great sorrow which distressed her terribly. She spent a night of agony without shedding a tear in case her reddened eyes gave her away. Her face was untroubled when she greeted me and she talked to me just as usual, even more charmingly if that were possible. I said to her quite simply: "I am sure you are suffering." She looked at me with unutterable astonishment . . . her bewilderment was so great that it affected me with an indefinable feeling of the supernatural. I felt God was there, very near to us. Quite without knowing it—for I have no gift of reading souls—I had spoken as if inspired and I was able to relieve her distress completely.

Now, dear Mother, I am going to tell you the greatest spiritual benefit I got from the novices. As you know, they are quite free to say whatever they think—good or bad. This is much easier for them with me as they do not owe me the respect due to a novice mistress.

I cannot say that Jesus gives me any outward, visible humiliations. He is content to humiliate me in the depths of my soul. I am apparently a complete success. I walk along the dangerous road of honours—if I can use such a phrase about convent life. And I understand why God and my superiors allow it. If the community thought I was an incompetent nun, with no brains or judgement, it would be impossible for you, Mother, to let me help you. That is why the divine Master has flung a veil over all my faults.

Because of this veil, the novices praise me. It is not flattery, for I know they really believe what they say. But their praise does not make me vain, for the knowledge of my wretchedness never leaves me for a moment. But sometimes, I have a great longing to hear something different from praise, for my soul sickens of too sweet a diet. It is then that Jesus gives me a nice little salad seasoned with vinegar and spice. The only thing missing is *olive oil*, and that makes it even tastier.

The novices offer me this salad when I least expect it. God raises the veil which hides my imperfections from them, and my dear little sisters then see the reality and no longer find me quite to their liking. With a simplicity I find charming, they tell me what a trial I am to them and what they find unpleasant about me. They stand on no more ceremony than if they were discussing someone else, for they know that their freedom of speech delights me.

It is actually more than delight. It is like a wonderful festival which overwhelms me with joy. If I had not experienced it, I could not believe that something so against one's natural feelings could afford such happiness.

Once when I was passionately longing to be humiliated, a

young postulant did it so effectively that I remembered when Semei cursed David and I repeated to myself the words of the holy king: "Yea, it is the Lord who hath bidden him say all these things."

This is how God looks after me. He cannot always offer me the nourishing bread of outward humiliation, but from time to time He lets me eat "the crumbs under the table of the children." How great is His mercy!

Dear Mother, as even in this world I am trying to sing with you of this infinite mercy, I must tell you of another real gain of mine which came like so many others from my little task. Before, whenever I saw a sister doing something I did not like and which seemed contrary to the rule, I would say: "Oh, how pleased I should be if I could warn her and show her her faults." But since that has been my job, my feelings have changed. When I happen to see something amiss, I give a sigh of relief: "How nice! She isn't a novice and I need not reprove her." I quickly try to find an excuse for her and endow her with all the good intentions she undoubtedly has.

Reverend Mother, I have learnt a great deal about charity from the care you have given me during my illness. No remedy has been too expensive, and if it did no good, you tired yourself out finding another. When I go to recreation, you go to endless trouble to place me out of the slightest draught. I feel, Mother, that I must have as much sympathy for the spiritual infirmities of my sisters as you have for my illness.

I have noticed that the holiest nuns are the most loved. Other people want to talk to them and perform unasked services for them. So these nuns find themselves loved by all, although they would not mind being neglected and treated without consideration. The words of our Father, St. John of the Cross, can be applied to them: "All good things have come to me since I no longer seek them for myself."

But imperfect souls have no friends. They are treated with the ordinary politeness of convent life but they are avoided, for one is afraid of saying something unfriendly. When I talk of imperfect souls, I am not referring only to spiritual imperfections, for the holiest person will be perfect only in heaven. I also have in mind such things as lack of judgement and education and a general touchiness of disposition. They are all things which do nothing to make life pleasant. I am well aware that these are chronic disabilities and there is no hope of curing them, but I am also aware that you, Mother, would not stop caring for me and trying to ease my sufferings if I remained ill for years.

From all this I have come to the conclusion that I should seek the company of those sisters for whom I have no natural liking and be like the good Samaritan to them. A word and a pleasant smile are often enough to cheer up someone who is sad and upset. But I want to be charitable not only to comfort people. I know I should soon lose heart if that were my aim, for something uttered with the best of intentions can, perhaps, be completely misunderstood. Therefore, to save time and trouble, I try to act solely to please Our Lord and to obey the Gospel: "When thou makest a dinner or a supper, call not thy friends nor thy brethren, lest perhaps they also invite thee again, and a recompense be made to thee. But when thou makest a feast, call the poor, the maimed, the lame and the blind; and thou shalt be blessed, because they have naught wherewith to make thee recompense: And thy Father who seeth in secret will repay thee." But what kind of a feast can I offer to my sisters except a spiritual one of loving, cheerful charity? I do not know any other kind and I want to be like St. Paul who rejoiced with those whom he found rejoicing. It is true he wept with the sorrowful and sometimes there will have to be tears at the feast I want to provide, but I shall always do my best to change these tears to smiles, for "God loveth the cheerful giver."

I remember an act of charity which God inspired me to perform while I was still a novice. It seemed a tiny act, but God "who seeth in secret" has already rewarded me for it in this life. It happened before Sister St. Peter became quite helpless. At ten to six every evening someone had to leave evening prayers to take her to the refectory. I was most reluctant to volunteer for this task, as I knew it was hard or rather impossible to please this poor sick nun. Yet it was a great chance for me and I did not want to let it slip, for I remembered Our Lord's words: "As long as you did it to one of these my least brethren, you did it to Me."

I offered to escort her. I was very humble about it, but it was not easy to persuade her to accept my help. I tackled the job with such willingness that I managed it perfectly in the end. Every evening, as soon as I saw her start shaking her hourglass, I knew it meant: "Let's start." Screwing up my courage, I got up and then quite a ceremony began. Before we set out, her stool had to be picked up and carried in a particular way. Above all, there had to be no sign of haste: I had to follow her, supporting her by her girdle, and I was as gentle as possible. If, however, she unfortunately stumbled, she instantly thought I was not holding on to her properly and that she was going to fall: "Oh, good heavens! You are walking too fast. I shall tumble down." Then, if I tried to lead her more slowly, I would hear: "Keep close to me. I can't feel your hand. You've let go. I'm going to fall! I knew very well you were far too young to look after me." We would finally arrive in the refectory without any accident. Fresh troubles began there. I had to settle the poor invalid in her place and it had to be done carefully so as not to hurt her. Her sleeves had to be turned back too, again in a particular way. That done, I could go.

But I soon noticed that she found it very difficult to cut her bread, and so I used not to leave her without doing it for her. She was very touched by this, as she had never asked me to do it. I won her complete trust through this and especially—as I discovered much later—because at the end of all my little duties I gave her what she called "my nicest smile."

It is a very long time, Mother, since this happened, yet Our Lord has left me a fragrant memory of it—like a breath from heaven. One winter evening I was as usual doing the humble task I have just described. It was cold and dark. Suddenly I heard away in the distance the music of a small orchestra and I pictured to myself a richly furnished and decorated drawing room, glowing with light and containing fashionably dressed young women exchanging worldly compliments. Then I looked at the poor invalid I was guiding along. Instead of music, I heard her pitiful complaints; instead of elegant decoration, I saw the bare bricks of our cloister in a faint glimmer of light. This contrast moved me. Our Lord poured on it that light of truth which so outshines the false glitter of earthly pleasures that I would not have given up the ten minutes it took for me to perform my act of charity in exchange for a thousand years of such worldly parties.

Now we suffer and are in the midst of our struggles and yet we can feel such delight at thinking that God has withdrawn us from the world, so what shall we feel in heaven when, surrounded by eternal glory and endless peace, we can realise how incomparable was the favour He did us in choosing us to dwell in this convent, His house and the gateway to heaven?

I have not always been so enraptured by practising charity, but at the start of my convent life Jesus wanted to make me feel how sweet it was to see Him in the souls of His spouses. And so I guided Sister St. Peter to the refectory with so much love that I could have done no better if I had been guiding Our Lord Himself.

As you will soon see, dear Mother, being charitable has not always been so pleasant for me, and to prove it I am going to tell you a few of my struggles. And they are not the only ones. At meditation I was for a long time always near a sister who never stopped fidgetting, with either her rosary or something else. Perhaps I was the only one who heard her, as my ears are very sharp, but I could not tell you how it irritated me. What I wanted to do was to turn and stare at her until she stopped her noise, but deep down I knew it was better to endure it patiently—first, for the love of God and, secondly, so as not to upset her. So I made no fuss, though sometimes I was soaked with sweat under the strain and my prayer was nothing but the prayer of suffering. At last I tried to find some way of enduring this suffering calmly and even joyfully. So I did my best to enjoy this unpleasant little noise. Instead of trying not to hear it—which was impossible—I strove to listen to it carefully as if it were a first-class concert, and my meditation, *which was not the prayer of quiet*, was spent in offering this concert to Jesus.

Another time I was in the washhouse near a sister who constantly splashed me with dirty water as she washed the handkerchiefs. My first impulse was to draw back and wipe my face so as to show her I would like her to work with less splashing. Then I at once thought how foolish I was to refuse the precious gifts offered me so generously and I was very careful not to show my annoyance. In fact, I made such efforts to want to be showered with dirty water that after half an hour I had genuinely taken a fancy to this novel kind of aspersion, and I decided to turn up as often as I could to that lucky spot where so much spiritual wealth was freely handed out.

You see, Mother, that I am a *very little* soul who can only offer *very little* things to God; it often happens that I let slip the chance of making these little sacrifices which give such peace, but I'm not discouraged. I put up with having a bit less peace and try to be more careful next time. Ah! How happy God makes me! It is so pleasant and easy to serve Him during this life. Yes, I shall always go on saying that He has given me what I wanted, or rather, that He has made me want what He wished to give me. For instance, just before my terrible temptation against faith I said: "I really have no outward troubles and God would have to change the path I tread for me to have any spiritual trials. I do not believe that He will. Yet I cannot always live in peace like this. So what will He do?"

I had not long to wait for the answer. It showed me that He I love is never stuck for ways and means. Without altering my path, He gave me that great trial which soon introduced a wholesome bitterness into all the sweetness of my life.

It is not only when He intends to send me some trial that Jesus makes me long for what is to come. For a very long time I had cherished a wish which seemed as if it could never be fulfilled: it was to have a brother a priest. I often thought that if my little brothers had not died, I should have had the joy of seeing them at the altar. It was a joy I regretted missing. I wanted only one brother as a priest who would remember me at the altar every day, but now God, going beyond my dream, linked my by spiritual bonds to *two* of His apostles. I want to tell you, dear Mother, just how God answered my prayer.

It was our Mother St. Teresa who sent me my first brother as a present for my feast day in 1895. It was washday and I was very busy when Mother Agnes of Jesus, who was then prioress, took me aside and read me a letter from a young seminarist. He said that he had been inspired by St. Teresa to ask for a sister who would devote herself specially to his salvation and to the salvation of the souls he would be dealing with in the future. He promised that in his Mass he would always remember the nun who became his spiritual sister. And I was the one chosen to be the sister of this future missionary.

I cannot tell you, Mother, how happy I was. The unexpected fulfilment of my longing awoke in me a joy that I can only call childlike, for I must go back to my childhood days to remember pleasure so great. My heart was too small to hold it. For years I had never experienced this sort of happiness. I felt as if my soul had been reborn and as if some of its neglected strings had been touched.

I understood my new obligations and set to work to fulfil them. I tried to increase my fervour and wrote several letters to my new brother. It is true that one can help missionaries by prayer and sacrifice, but sometimes Jesus chooses to link together two souls for His glory and then He lets them exchange their thoughts to stir each other to a greater love of God. But one must be expressly requested to do this by one's superiors; such a correspondence would do more harm than good if one asked for it—if not to the missionary, at least to the Carmelite who should live retired within herself. An exchange of letters, even if infrequent, would busy her mind uselessly rather than unite her to God. Perhaps she would imagine she was achieving wonders, although actually doing nothing but, under the cloak of zeal, providing herself with unnecessary distraction.

Here I am again, dear Mother, involved not in a distraction but in a sermon which is equally superfluous. I shall never correct myself of this wordiness which must be very boring for you to have to read! Forgive me, even if I start off again at the first opportunity.

At the end of May last year it was your turn to give me my second brother. When I said that as I had already offered my slight merits for a future apostle, I did not think I could make them available for another, you told me that obedience would double their value. In my heart I was sure of it, and since the zeal of a Carmelite should embrace the world, I even hope, by the grace of God, to help more than two missionaries. I pray for everyone and do not forget ordinary priests whose ministry is sometimes just as difficult as that of missionaries preaching to the heathen. Like our Mother, St. Teresa, I want to be "a daughter of the Church" and pray for all the intentions of Christ's Vicar. It is the great aim of my life.

If my own dear brothers had lived, I should have been specially concerned with their work without neglecting, because of that, the general interests of the Church which cover the whole universe. In exactly the same way, I am specially united to the new brothers given me by Jesus. All I have belongs equally to each of them, for God is too good and generous to divide it. He is so rich that He gives me without limit what I ask, although I do not get involved in making up a long catalogue of my wants. As I have two brothers and the novices, the days would not be long enough for me to detail the needs of each soul, and in any case I should be terrified of forgetting something important. Complicated methods are no use to simple souls, and as I am one of those, Our Lord Himself has given me a very simple little means of fulfilling my obligations.

After Holy Communion one day He made me understand the significance of these words in the Canticle of Canticles: "Draw me: we will run after Thee to the odour of Thy ointments." So, Jesus, there is no need to say: In drawing me, draw also the souls I love. The simple words "Draw me" are enough! When a soul has been captivated by the intoxicating odour of Your ointments, she cannot run alone. Every soul she loves is drawn after her—a natural consequence of her being drawn to You.

As a river sweeps along it carries with it all it meets down to the depths of the sea, and so, my Jesus, the soul which plunges into the boundless ocean of Your love carries with it all its treasures. You know that my treasures are those souls which You have linked with mine. You have entrusted these treasures to me and so I dare borrow Your own words, those You used on the last evening You spent as a mortal traveller on earth.

Jesus, my Beloved, I do not know when my exile will end. Perhaps I shall spend many evenings here below still singing of Your mercy, but in the end the last evening will come . . . and then I want to be able to say to You: "I have glorified Thee on earth: I have finished the work which Thou gavest me to do. I have manifested Thy Name to the men whom Thou hast given me out of the world. Thine they were, and to me thou gavest them; and they have kept Thy Word. Now they have known that all things which Thou hast given me are from Thee: because the words which Thou gavest me I have given to them; and they have received them, and have known in very deed that I came forth from Thee, and they have believed that Thou didst send me. I pray for them: I pray not for the world, but for them whom Thou hast given me, because they are Thine. And all mine are Thine, and Thine are mine; and I am glorified in them. And now I am not in the world, and these are in the world, and I come to Thee. Holy Father, keep them in Thy name, whom Thou hast given me, that they may be one, as we also are one. And now I come to Thee, and these things I speak in the world, that they may have my joy filled in themselves. I do not ask that Thou take them away out of the world, but that Thou keep them from evil. They are not of the world, as I am not of the world. And not for them only do I pray, but for them also who through their word shall believe in me. Father, I will that where I am, they also whom Thou hast given me may be with me; that they may see my glory which Thou hast given me, because Thou hast loved me before the creation of the world. And I have made known Thy Name unto them, and will make it known; that the love wherewith Thou hast loved me may be in them and I in them."

Yes, Lord, those are the words I want to repeat before I fly to Your arms. Perhaps I am being presumptuous . . . no, of course not . . . for a long time You have let me be bold and free with You. You have said to me what the prodigal son's father said to his elder son: "All I have is thine." So Your words, Jesus, are mine and I can use them to draw down the Heavenly Father's favours on to the souls which belong to me.

You know, God, that I have never wanted anything but to love You alone. I long for no other glory. Your love has gone before me from my childhood, it has grown with me, and now it is an abyss whose depths I cannot plumb. Love attracts love and mine soars up to You, eager to fill the abyss of Your love, but it is not even a drop of dew lost in the ocean. To love You as You love me, I must borrow Your love—only then can I have peace. O Jesus, it seems to me that You cannot give a soul more love than You have bestowed on me, and that is why I dare ask You to love those You have given me "even as You have loved me." If, one day in heaven, I find out that You love them more than me, I shall rejoice, recognising that even on earth they must have deserved it more, but meanwhile I cannot imagine any greater love than that You have given me without any merit of my own.

I am astounded, Mother, at what I have just written. I did not mean to!

When I repeated this passage from the Gospel: "The words which Thou gavest me I have given unto them," I was not thinking of my brothers but of my sisters in the noviciate, for I do not consider myself able to instruct missionaries. For them I wrote these words from the prayer of Jesus: "I do not ask that Thou shouldst take them out of the world. . . . I prayed also for them who through their Lord shall believe in Thee." For how could I forget the souls they will win through their suffering and their preaching?

But I have said all I think about these words from the Canticle of Canticles: "Draw me—we will run."

Jesus said: "No man can come to me except the Father who has sent me draw him." Later He teaches us that we have only to knock and it will be opened, to seek and we shall find, to hold out our hand humbly to receive. He adds: "If you ask the Father anything in my Name He will give it you." And that, no doubt, is why the Holy Spirit, long before the birth of Jesus, dictated this prophetic prayer: "Draw me—we will run." When we ask to be drawn, we are wanting to be closely united with the object which has won our heart. If fire and iron could reason and if the iron said to the fire: "Draw me," that would prove its wish to be so identified with the fire as to share its very substance. Well, that is just what my prayer is. I ask Jesus to draw me into the flames of His love and to unite me so closely to Him that He lives and acts in me. I feel that the more the fire of love encompasses my heart, the more I shall say: "Draw me," and the more will those souls who are near to mine "run swiftly in the sweet odour of the Beloved." Yes, they will run and we shall run together, for souls on fire cannot stay still. Like St. Magdalene, they may sit at the feet of Jesus, listening to His gentle yet exciting words. They seem to give Him nothing, yet they give much more than Martha who is anxious "about many things." Jesus does not, of course, blame Martha's work, but only her worrying about it. For His Mother humbly did the same jobs when she got the meals ready for the Holy Family.

This lesson has been understood by all the saints, perhaps especially by those who have illumined the world with the teaching of the Gospels. Was it not in prayer that St. Paul, St. Augustine, St. Thomas of Aquinas, St. John of the Cross, St. Teresa, and so many other friends of God found that wonderful knowledge which has enraptured the greatest intellects? Archimedes said: "Give me a fulcrum and with a lever I will move the world." What he could not get, the saints have been given. The Almighty has given them a fulcrum: Himself, Himself alone. For a lever they have that prayer which burns with the fire of love. Thus they have moved the world, and it is with this lever that those still battling in the world move it and will go on moving it till the end of time.

Dear Mother, I have still to tell you what I understand by "the sweet odour of the Beloved." Since Jesus has gone to heaven, I can follow Him only by the traces He has left. But how radiant and how fragrant these traces are! I have only to glance at the Holy Gospels and at once I breathe the fragrance of His life and know which way to run. I rush to the lowest place, not the highest. I leave the Pharisee to go ahead, and repeat, with the greatest confidence, the humble prayer of the publican. Above all I imitate Mary Magdalene, for her amazing—or rather her loving—audacity which won the Heart of Jesus captivates mine.

It is not because I have been preserved from mortal sin that I fly to God with loving confidence. I know I should still have this confidence even if my conscience were burdened with every possible crime. I should fling myself into the arms of my Saviour, heartbroken with sorrow. I know how He loved the prodigal son, I have heard His words to St. Mary Magdalene, to the woman taken in adultery, and to the woman of Samaria. No, no one could frighten me, for I know what to think about His love and His mercy. I know that a host of sins would vanish in the twinkling of an eye like a drop of water flung into a furnace.

In the lives of the Desert Fathers there is a story about one of them who converted a sinner whose behaviour had shocked the whole countryside. Touched by grace, she followed the saint into the desert to perform a severe penance. On the first night of the journey, before she even reached her retreat, the violence of her repentance and her love killed her, and at that moment the hermit saw the angels carry her soul to God.

That is a very striking example of what I want to say, but these things cannot be put into words.

CHAPTER ELEVEN

You, my dearest sister, have asked me to leave you a souvenir. The Reverend Mother has given me permission, so it's with joy that I talk to you who are really doubly my sister. For when I was too young to speak, you promised in my name that I would serve no one but Jesus. Dear, dear Godmother, it's the baby you offered to God who is speaking to you now. I love you just as a baby loves its mother, and it's only in heaven that you'll understand just how grateful I am to you.

You want to know, darling sister, what secrets Jesus has entrusted to me, your little daughter. Yet I know you also know these secrets, for you were the one who taught me to listen to His teaching. However, I'm going to try to stammer out a few words, although it's impossible to clothe in language things the heart can hardly grasp.

Don't imagine that I'm overwhelmed with consolations. I'm not. My consolation is not to have any in this life. Jesus never manifests Himself nor lets me hear His voice. He teaches me in secret. I never learn anything from books, for I don't understand what I read. Yet from time to time a sentence comforts me. This evening, after a barren period of meditation, I read this: "Here is the Master I give you. He will teach you all you need to do. I want to make you read of the *science of love* in the book of life." The science of love! The words echo sweetly through my soul. It is the only thing I want to know. Like the spouse in the Canticle of Canticles, "having given up all the substance of my house for love, I reckon it as nothing." I long for no other treasure but love, for it alone can make us pleasing to God.

Jesus has shown me the only path which leads to this divine furnace of love. It is the complete abandonment of a baby sleeping without a fear in its father's arms. "Whoever is a little one, let him come unto Me," the Holy Ghost has said through Solomon's mouth. In His name the prophet Isaias reveals that on the last day the Lord "shall feed His flock like a shepherd: He shall gather together the lambs with His arm, and shall take them up in His bosom." And if this is not enough, the same prophet cries in the name of the Lord: "You shall be carried at the breasts and upon the knees they shall caress you. As one whom the mother caresseth, so will I comfort you."

Oh, dearest, dearest sister, what is there to do after such words but stay still and weep with gratitude and love? If people who are as weak and imperfect as I am only felt what I feel, not one of them would despair of scaling the summit of the mountain of love. Jesus does not demand great deeds. All He wants is self-surrender and gratitude. "I will not take he-goats out of thy flocks, for all the beasts of the forest are Mine, the cattle on the hills and the oxen. I know all the fowls of the air. If I were hungry, I would not tell thee, for the world is Mine, and the fulness thereof. Shall I eat the flesh of bullocks, or shall I drink the blood of goats? OFFER TO GOD THE SACRIFICE OF PRAISE AND THANKSGIVING."

That is all Jesus asks from us. He needs nothing from us except our love. God, who declares He has no need to tell us He is hungry, does not hesitate to *beg* a drop of water from the woman of Samaria. . . . He was thirsty!!! But when He said: "Give me to drink," the Creator of the universe was asking for the love of the poor thing He had created. He was thirsty for love! And now more than ever Jesus thirsts. From the worldly He meets with only in-gratitude and indifference, and even among His disciples there are very few who surrender fully to the tenderness of His infinite love.

How happy we both are to be able to understand the secrets of Jesus! If you would write what you know of them, what wonderful pages we should read. But I know you prefer to keep "the secrets of the King" to yourself. You tell me "it is honourable to reveal and confess the works of God," yet I think you are right to keep silent, for it is quite impossible to describe the secrets of heaven in the words of earth.

As far as I am concerned, I should feel I had not even begun no matter how many pages I wrote. There are such wide horizons and so many infinite aspects that, after the night of this life is over, only the palette of the divine Painter will be able to supply the colours I need to paint the wonders He reveals to my inward eye.

Yet, my darling sister, since you want to know as much as possi-ble of my deepest feelings and want me to write about the most comforting dream of my life and about what you call "my little doctrine," I will obey. I shall speak to Jesus and He will help me to express myself. Perhaps you'll find my words exaggerated, but I assure you there's no excitement or exaggeration in my heart: it is calm and quite at peace.

How can I describe, Jesus, how gently and tenderly you guide me? A great storm had raged furiously within me since Easter, the radiant feast of Your triumph, until, on a day in May, You sent a serene ray of grace through my gloom.

I had often thought of the mysterious dreams You sometimes grant those You favour, but I told myself such comfort was not for me. Night, pitch-black unchanging night, was my fate. I slept amid the storm.

At dawn next morning, May 10, I dreamt I was in the corridor, walking alone with Reverend Mother. Suddenly, without knowing how they had got there, I saw three Carmelite nuns, wearing their mantles and long veils. I knew they were from heaven. "How happy I should be," I thought, "to see the face of one of them." As if my wish had been heard, the tallest of them walked towards me. I knelt. She lifted her veil or rather covered us both with it. Instantly I recognised the Venerable Mother Anne of Jesus, the foundress of Carmel in France. Her face had a beauty not of this earth; no ray of light shone from it, and yet, in spite of the thick veil which covered us both, I saw her face lit by a gentle glow.

She caressed me and, moved by her love, I ventured to say: "I implore you, Mother, to tell me if God is going to leave me on earth for long. Will He come for me soon?" She gave me a tender smile: "Yes, soon . . . soon. I promise you." I went on: "Tell me also, Mother, if God is pleased with me. Does He want anything from me beyond my poor little deeds and longings?" As I spoke, her face shone with a new splendour and her gaze grew even more tender. She said: "God asks nothing more from you. He is pleased, very pleased." She took my head between her hands and I cannot give you any idea of the sweetness of her love for me. I was aflame with joy, but I thought of my sisters and wanted to ask some favours for them. But I woke up. This dream made me indescribably happy, and although several months have passed, its freshness and heavenly charm are still sharp in my memory. I can still see the smiling gaze, so full of love, of that holy Carmelite and I imagine I can still feel her embracing me.

When I woke from this dream, I believed and I knew that heaven exists and that souls dwell there who love me and look upon me as their child. The realisation of this never left me, and it was all the sweeter because until then I had been quite indifferent to the Venerable Mother Anne of Jesus. I never thought of her unless I heard someone speak of her, and that was not very often. But now I know and really understand that she is far from indifferent about me. This knowledge deepens my love both for her and for all the blessed ones in heaven.

O my Beloved! This grace was only the prelude of the greater ones You wished to shower on me. Let me recall them to You, and forgive me if I talk nonsense in trying to tell You again about those hopes and desires of mine which are almost limitless . . . forgive me and heal my soul by granting it what it wants. It should be enough for me, Jesus, to be Your spouse, to be a Carmelite and, by union with You, to be the mother of souls. Yet I long for other vocations: I want to be a warrior, a priest, an apostle, a doctor of the Church, a martyr. . . . I would like to perform the most heroic deeds. I feel I have the courage of a Crusader. I should like to die on the battlefield in defence of the Church.

If only I were a priest! How lovingly, Jesus, would I hold You in my hands when my words had brought You down from heaven and how lovingly would I give You to the faithful. Yet though I long to be a priest, I admire and envy the humility of St. Francis of

Assisi and feel that I should imitate him and refuse the sublime dignity of the priesthood. How can I reconcile these desires?

Like the prophets and the doctors of the Church, I should like to enlighten souls. I should like to wander through the world, preaching Your Name and raising Your glorious Cross in pagan lands. But it would not be enough to have only one field of mission work. I should not be satisfied unless I preached the Gospel in every quarter of the globe and even in the most remote islands. Nor should I be content to be a missionary for only a few years. I should like to have been one from the creation of the world and to continue as one till the end of time. But, above all, I long to be a martyr. From my childhood I have dreamt of martyrdom, and it is a dream which has grown more and more real in my little cell in Carmel. But I don't want to suffer just one torment. I should have to suffer them all to be satisfied. Like you, my adorable Jesus, I want to be scourged and crucified. I want to be flayed like St. Bartholomew. Like St. John, I want to be flung into boiling oil. Like St. Ignatius of Antioch, I long to be ground by the teeth of wild beasts, ground into a bread worthy of God. With St. Agnes and St. Cecilia, I want to offer my neck to the sword of the executioner and, like Joan of Arc, murmur the name of Jesus at the stake. My heart leaps when I think of the unheard tortures Christians will suffer in the reign of anti-Christ. I want to endure them all. My Jesus, fling open that book of life in which are set down the deeds of every saint. I want to perform them all for You!

Now what can You say to all my silliness? Is there anywhere in the world a tinier, weaker soul than mine? Yet just because I am so weak, You have granted my little, childish desires and now You will grant those desires of mine which are far vaster than the universe. These desires caused me a real martyrdom, and so one day I opened the epistles of St. Paul to try to find some cure for my sufferings.

And in chapters twelve and thirteen of the First Epistle to the Corinthians I read that we cannot all be apostles, prophets, and doctors, that the Church is made up of different members, and that the eye cannot also be the hand. This answer was clear enough, but it did not satisfy me and brought me no peace. But as St. John of the Cross says, "descending into the depths of my own nothingness, I was raised so high that I reached my goal." I went on reading and came to: "Be zealous for the better gifts. And I show unto you a yet more excellent way." The apostle explains how even all the most perfect gifts are nothing without love and that charity is the most excellent way of going safely to God. I had found peace at last.

I thought of the Mystical Body of the Church, but I could not recognise myself in any of its members listed by St. Paul—or, rather, I wanted to recognise myself in them all. Charity gave me the key to *my vocation*. I realised that if the Church was a body made up of different members, she would not be without the greatest and most essential of them all. I realised that love includes all vocations, that love is all things, and that, because it is eternal, it embraces every time and place.

Swept by an ecstatic joy, I cried: "Jesus, my love! At last I have found my vocation. My vocation is love! I have found my place in the bosom of the Church and it is You, Lord, who has given it me. In the heart of the Church, who is my Mother, *I will be love*. So I shall be everything and so my dreams will be fulfilled!" Why do I speak of "ecstatic joy"? It's the wrong phrase to use. Instead, I should speak of peace, that calm, tranquil peace which the helmsman feels as he sees the beacon which guides him into harbour. How brightly this beacon of love burns! And I know how to reach it and how to make its flames my own.

I am only a weak and helpless child, yet it is my very weakness which has made me daring enough to offer myself to You, Jesus, as the victim of Your love. Long ago only pure and spotless victims were accepted by Almighty God. The divine justice could be satisfied only by immaculate victims, but the law of love has replaced that of fear, and love has chosen me as victim—feeble and imperfect creature that I am. Is the choice of me worthy of love? Yes, it is, because in order for love to be fully satisfied it must descend to nothingness and transform that nothingness to living fire. I know, Lord, that "love is repaid by love alone." And so I have sought and I have found the way to ease my heart—by giving You love for love.

"Use the riches that make men unjust, to find yourselves friends who may receive you into everlasting dwellings." This is the advice You gave to Your disciples after You had told them that "the children of this world are wiser in their generation than the children of light." As a child of light, I saw that my longings to be all things and to embrace every vocation could easily make me unjust. So I used them to make friends for myself. I remembered the prayer of Eliseus to the prophet Elias, and so I stood before the angels and the assembly of saints and said: "I am the smallest of creatures and I recognise my worthlessness, but I also know how hearts that are generous and noble love to do good. So I beseech you, happy dwellers in heaven, to adopt me as your child. The glory you will enable me to win will be yours. Please answer my prayer! I implore you to let me have a double portion of your love of God!"

O Lord, I cannot fathom the full implication of my prayer. I know that if I could, I should be afraid of being crushed by its rashness. But my excuse is that I am a child and children don't think what their words mean. But if a father and mother sat on a throne and possessed immense wealth, they would not hesitate to grant the desires of their little children, for they love them more than themselves. To please their children, such parents would do foolish things. Well, I am the child of the Church and the Church is a queen because, O King of Kings, she is Your Bride. My heart has no desire for riches or glory, even the glory of heaven. That glory belongs by right to my brothers—the angels and the saints. My own glory is a reflection of that which shines from the brow of my Mother, the Church. But what I demand is love. I care now about one thing only—to love You, my Jesus! Great deeds are forbidden me, I cannot preach the Gospel nor shed my blood—but what does it matter? My brothers toil instead of me and I, a little child, well, I keep close by the throne of God and I *love* for those who fight. Love proves itself by deeds, so how am I to show my love? Well, I will scatter flowers, perfuming the divine Throne with their fragrance, and I'll sweetly sing my hymn of love. Yes, my Beloved, that is how I'll spend my short life. The only way I can prove my love is by scattering flowers and these flowers are every little sacrifice, every glance and word, and the doing of the least of actions for love. I wish both to suffer and to find joy through love. Thus will I scatter my flowers. I will never find one without plucking its petals for You and I shall sing, sing without ceasing even if I have to gather my roses from the midst of thorns. And the longer and sharper the thorns, the sweeter my song will be.

I wonder, Jesus, what use You will have for my songs and flowers. I know that these frail and worthless petals and the songs of love from one so tiny will nevertheless please You. Yes, indeed, these trifles will give You pleasure. So they will the Church Triumphant who, wishing to play with her little child, will gather up the rose petals. Then, after giving them infinite worth by placing them in Your hands, she will fling them on to the Church Suffering to extinguish the flames which threaten her, and on to the Church Militant to ensure her victory.

Jesus, I love you, and I love the Church my Mother. I remember that "the smallest act of love is more to her than every other work put together." But is my heart really full of this pure love? Are my limitless desires a dream, a piece of foolishness? If they are, tell me, for You know I want the truth. If my desires are rash, take them away, for they are a most terrible martyrdom. Yet I confess that even if I never enter these high realms to which my soul aspires, I shall have known more sweetness in my martyrdom and in my folly than I shall ever know in the midst of eternal joy. That is, unless by a miracle You wiped from my memory the hopes I had while on earth. Jesus, my Jesus, if this longing for love is so wonderful, what will it be like actually to possess and enjoy it forever? How can a soul as imperfect as mine hope for love in all its fulness? Why do You keep these boundless longings for great souls, those eagles which soar to the heights? I, alas, am only a poor little unfledged bird. I am not an eagle. All I have are the eyes and the heart of one, for in spite of my littleness I dare gaze at the Sun of love and long to fly towards it. I want to fly and imitate the eagles, but all I can do is flap my tiny wings. They are too weak to lift me. What shall I do? Die of grief at being so helpless. Oh no! I shan't even let it trouble me. With cheerful confidence I shall stay gazing at the Sun until I die. Nothing will frighten me, neither wind nor rain. If thick clouds hide the Sun and if it seems that nothing exists beyond the night of this life—well, then, that will be a moment of *perfect joy,* a moment to feel complete trust and stay very still, secure in the knowledge that my adorable Sun still shines behind the clouds.

O God, I do understand Your love for me, but, as You know, I very often let myself be turned aside from the only thing I care about. I stay away from You and soil my half-formed wings in the dirty puddles of the world. Then "I cry like a young swallow" and my cry tells You all and, in Your infinite mercy, You remember that You did "not come to call the just, but sinners." Yet if You refuse to heed the plaintive cries of Your feeble creature, if You remain hidden, I shall just stay wet and numb with cold and again rejoice in my deserved suffering. O my beloved Sun, I delight in feeling small and helpless in Your presence and my heart is at peace . . . I know that all the eagles of heaven pity me, protect me, defend me, and drive off the vultures—the demons—who would destroy me. I have no fear of these vultures. I am not fated to become their prey, but that of the divine Eagle.

O eternal Word, my Saviour, You are the Eagle I love and the One who fascinates me. You swept down to this land of exile and suffered and died so that You could bear away every soul and plunge them into the heart of the Blessed Trinity, that inextinguishable furnace of love. You re-entered the splendours of heaven, yet stayed in our vale of tears hidden under the appearance of a white Host so that You can feed me with Your own substance. O Jesus, do not be angry if I tell You that Your love is a mad love . . . and how can You expect my heart, when confronted with this folly, not to soar up to You? How can there be any limit to my trust?

I know that for You the saints have also been foolish. Because they were eagles they have done great deeds. I am too small to do anything great, and so my folly is to hope that Your love will accept me as its victim; my folly is to rely on the angels and the saints so that I may fly to You, my adored Eagle, with Your own wings. For as long as You wish, I will stay with my eyes on You. I want to be *fascinated* by Your gaze. I want to be the prey of Your love. I hope that one day You will swoop down on me, carry me off to the furnace of love, and plunge me into its burning depths so that I can be its ecstatic victim for all eternity.

O Jesus, if only I could tell all *little souls* of Your immeasurable condescension. I feel that if You found a soul feebler than mine—though that's impossible—You would delight in heaping even greater favours on it if it abandoned itself with supreme confidence to Your infinite mercy.

But why do I want to tell the secrets of Your love, my Beloved? You alone have taught me them and surely You can reveal them to others. I know You can and I implore You to: *I beseech You to cast Your divine glance upon a vast number of little souls. I beg You to choose in this world a multitude of little victims worthy of Your LOVE!!!*

ABOUT THE AUTHOR

JOHN BEEVERS was a distinguished biographer of Saint Thérèsè and the author of the bestselling *Storm of Glory.* He was born in England in 1911, studied at Cambridge University, and was a long-standing member of the BBC, where he worked as a writer and journalist for many years. He spent the later part of his life in Norfolk, England. He died in Norfolk in 1975.